INSIGHT POCKET

KU-332-087

TURKISH COAST

APA PUBLICATIONS

L

Part of the Langenscheidt Publishing Group

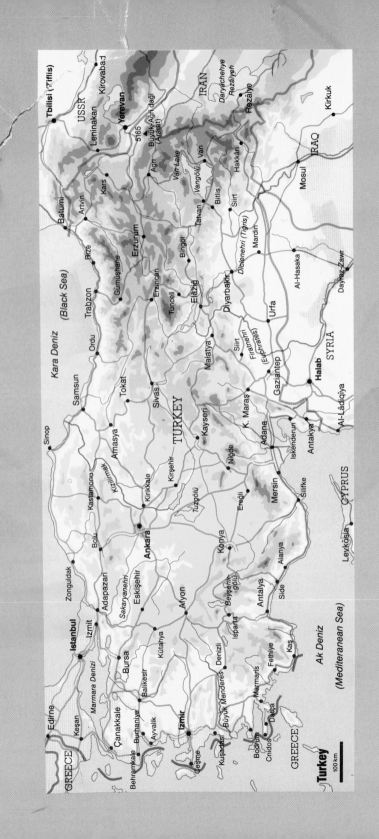

Welcome!

The Turkish Coast is associated with such famous historical figures as Alexander the Great, Antony and Cleopatra (for whom it was a romantic hideaway) and St Paul (Epistle to the Ephesians). Today it is a rewarding holiday destination, offering spectacular scenery, superb Classical sites and first-rate facilities for sailing, snorkelling and scuba diving.

In these pages Insight Guides' correspondent in Turkey, Metin Demirsar, brings you the best of the region. Fourteen full-day tours based on four key destinations – Bodrum, Marmaris, Fethiye and Antalya – work their way from west to east (though the journey works just as well in reverse). They include side-trips to places such as Ephesus north of Bodrum and Turtle Beach near Dalyan, as well as trips by boat to nearby islands. All tours include recommendations for rest and refreshment en route, and following the itineraries are sections on shopping, eating out, festivals and practical information. Though you are advised to hire a car for some of the itineraries, in particular the stretch between Dalaman and Alanya, excellent public transport – buses or 'dolmuş' – offers a viable alternative.

 Metin Demirsar is a journalist based in Istanbul, who has been visiting the Turkish Coast for both work and pleasure for over 20 years. He has witnessed enormous changes during that time, as fishing villages have expanded into full-blown resorts. Nonetheless he remains an ardent fan of the region, inspired by its history and archaeology and finding in its idyllic coves and harbourfront restaurants the perfect antidote to hectic Istanbul.

C O N T E N T S

Pages 2/3: beach at the Dead Sea

Pages 8/9:
women folk dancers

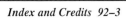

HISTORY & CULTURE

Long neglected by the Turkish government, the Turkish Coast emerged in the late 1980s as one of the world's leading travel destinations. Yet scratch the surface of this region and a rich mosaic of history and culture reveals itself. Some of the world's earliest civilisations thrived on its shores, including the Hittites, the Ionians, the Carians, the Lydians and the Lycians. The history of the Turkish Coast is replete with romantic encounters, mass migrations, violent invasions and bloody conquests. Persian armies, Roman legions, crusading knights and Muslim Turkish warriors have marched along the coast, each leaving their mark.

From Hittites to Lycians

Written records indicate that the Hittites were probably the first organised peoples to control the Turkish Coast, although the region was inhabited as early as 600,000BC by cave dwellers who had developed an advanced stone-chipping industry to produce arrow heads, scrapers and a variety of other simple utensils.

The Hittites invaded Anatolia between 2300–1900BC from the Caucasus or the Balkans and brought much of Central and Western Anatolia under the control of their capital at Hattush, in north-central Asia Minor. The feudal state was one of the principal powers in the Middle East until its defeat by the Assyrians in 717BC .

Beginning in the 13th century BC Anatolia was subjected to invasions by barbaric Indo-European tribes. Some of these, such as the Ionians, settled peacefully on the coast, taking on many of the customs and gods of the indigenous groups; others wreaked considerable destruction on the cities in their paths. The Hit-

Hittite lion

Ruins of Troy

tites and other local people, such as the Trojans, bore the brunt of the invasions and suffered heavily.

Thracian invaders – or Phrygians – were probably responsible for the sacking of Hattush around 1180BC, some 70 years after the destruction of Troy. They appeared on the coast around 1160BC and grew steadily more powerful on the eastern fringes of the region. Their contribution to life on the coast included the improvement of trade routes known as the Royal Roads, one of which ran east from Izmir through Dorylaeum (Eskişehir), Ankara and Boğazkale; another, slightly south, led from Sardis through central Anatolia and the Cilician Gates; both eventually ended at Susa, now a ruined city in western Iran. The Phrygians, best known for their King Midas, whose touch was said to turn everything into gold, built their capital in Gordium in northwest Anatolia.

Cimmerians from the Caucasus sacked Gordium around 690BC, bringing the Phrygian Empire to a close. The territory was then absorbed into the Lydian Empire, which made Sardis, near present-day Manisa, its capital. The Lydians, who controlled the coastal area for about 150 years, invented coin money as a medium of exchange. By occupying the Phrygian lands left unattended in the Cimmerians' wake, the Lydians came in contact with Persia and aroused the greedy envy of its kings. A Persian army under King Cyrus defeated the Lydians and conquered the coast, where independent Ionian, Carian and Lycian city states had emerged. They governed by means of local satraps (governors).

The Ionians had migrated from Greece sometime before 900BC. Their sphere of influence stretched from north of Izmir to Miletus in the south. During the 8th and 7th centuries BC they led the development of the Panionic League of 12 cities. They sent out a number of colonies to the shores of the Dardanelles, the Marmara and the Black Sea. Their cultural influence was also impressive: the temple of Diana in Ephesus was a masterpiece of Ionic architecture, and the Mausoleum in Halicarnassus (today's Bodrum) was considered among the Seven Wonders of the Ancient World.

The Lycians, an ancient people who raided Cyprus and fought the Hittites, Persians and Romans, had made the rugged mountainous area around Xanthus their home. Fiercely independent, they resisted all attempts at outside domination, often choosing mass suicide rather than subjugation by foreign powers. Many of their tombs dot the coast today.

The Carians were among the earliest inhabitants of the region

11

that now encompasses Muğla province. A native-stock Anatolian people, they were famed for their skills as mariners. Ancient chronicles say Carian sailors served in the navies of the Egyptian pharaohs and of the Persian ruler Xerxes. Mylasa and Halicarnassus were their main cities, Labraynda, their chief religious centre.

In 484BC, at the time of the Persian-Greek wars, Halicarnassus was ruled by a Carian dynasty whose most famous member was Queen Artemesia. When Xerxes, the Persian King of Kings, was preparing his invasion of Greece, Artemesia joined his forces, contributing several fighting ships. During a naval battle in 480BC in which the Persian fleet was routed, Artemesia displayed unusual bravery, causing Xerxes to exclaim: 'My men have shown themselves women and my women men.'

The golden age of the Carians was the reign of King Mausolus, a Persian-appointed satrap. Mausolus moved his capital from Mylasa to Halicarnassus, turning it into a splendid city. He built the city walls, part of which are still standing today, and relocated the populations of six Carian cities to Halicarnassus.

He died in 353BC and was succeeded by Artemesia the Younger, his wife and sister. Artemesia, who ruled for only three years, built a majestic tomb in her husband's memory (from which we get the word 'mausoleum'). She also gained fame as a naval strategist, defeating the invading Rhodians.

Greeks, Romans and Byzantines

Anatolia was under Persian control for about 200 years altogether, directed from Susa. In general, Persian rule was benign, with activities confined to recruiting soldiers and levying taxes.

The army of Alexander the Great swept through the Turkish coast in 334BC, liberating the Ionian Greek cities of Asia Minor from Persian yoke, in a campaign to build a world empire. Many coastal cities, including Ephesus, Side and Phaselis opened their doors to his army. In these cities, Alexander established Greek-style democracies in place of the oligarchies which had ruled under the Persians. After Alexander's death, the region came under the control of his generals, first Antigonus the One-Eyed and later of Lysmachus.

The era 323–30BC, known as the Hellenistic Age, was characterised by the collapse of the Greek city-states and the establishment of large kingdoms, modelled on the Macedonian monarchy. This period saw a

Phaselis Theatre

Battle detail on the sarcophagus of Alexander the Great

spectacular growth in trade as well as the development of a common culture made possible by use of the Greek language and the adoption of Greek institutions.

Roman legions first set foot in Asia Minor in 190BC for the purpose of defending Greece which was under attack from Antiochus III, head of the Seleucids, one of the dynasties that grew out of the vast empire of Alexander. For many years, Rome cultivated strong alliances with kingdoms in Anatolia, particularly Pergamum, to secure its boundaries, protect its interests in Asia Minor and act as a buffer state between Rome and the Seleucid Empire. Pergamum's military support was essential in Rome's campaigns in Greece and Asia Minor and victory at the final Battle of Magnesia, *Local goddess* which put an end to Seleucid rule in Asia Minor. As a result of the victory, Rome acquired the vast territory ruled by Antiochus III.

The Romans handed over the administration of Asia Minor to the Pergamum kingdom, under the condition that it adhered to Rome's foreign policy. This relationship ensured that western Asia Minor was governed in the interest of Rome but the responsibility of rule lay with the Pergamene kings.

In 133BC, the last Pergamene king, Attalus III, bequeathed the royal possessions of Pergamum and the supremacy of western Asia Minor to Rome.

Through direct contacts with the Greeks in Asia Minor, Romans were greatly influenced by the Greek religion and culture and were fascinated by Greek literature and philosophy. They translated Homer, and copied its forms in writing the epic histories of Rome. The children of upper-class Roman families learned to speak and read Greek.

The founding of Constantinople as the new capital in AD330 by Emperor Constantine I (the Great) resulted in a shift of the imperial centre to the east. The permanent division of the Empire into east and west resulted in the gradual assimilation of Roman Asia Minor into the Graeco-Anatolian world. By the time the western Roman Empire had collapsed in the 5th century, the assimilation was

Yilankale, Crusader castle, Adana

complete. In place of the Latin Roman Empire stood the Greek-dominated Byzantine Empire, which was to last until the Ottoman conquest in the 15th century.

Beginning with Antioch in about AD40, under the influence of St Paul and the early disciples Christianity spread thoughout the eastern Mediterranean. Three centuries later Christianity had become the major religion of Asia Minor.

Enter the Turks

In 1070, the Seljuk Turks, a nomadic warrior race originating from the steppes of Central Asia and bearing the banner of Islam, captured Jerusalem. In the following year they all but annihilated the Byzantine army at Malazgirt (Menzikert): the Byzantine Emperor, Romanus IV Diogenes, was taken prisoner. Within 20 years, the Seljuk armies had overrun most of Anatolia. Their power towered over the Bosphorus, casting a dark shadow over Constantinople itself (1092). The coast was now a firm Turkish possession.

Hoping to unify the divided Christian world and conquer the Holy Lands, the papacy sponsored a series of Crusades stretching over the next 370 years. Battles were fought along the coast, but the Crusaders failed to turn back the Turkish hordes.

In 1204, the rapacious Latin Crusaders sacked Constantinople, killed thousands of Orthodox Christians, destroyed many magnificent buildings and carted off priceless relics to Venice. The Byzantine emperors fled to nearby Nicaea, modern-day Iznik, and a Latin state was established in Constantinople. Although the Byzantine emperors recaptured Constantinople in 1261 and restored the enfeebled empire, the city never recovered from the plunder. Conditions were ripe for the Ottoman conquest.

The Ottomans started out as a tiny principality of the Seljuks.

Exploiting the rivalries of other Turkish princes and the weaknesses of the Byzantine Empire, they unified the Turks in Anatolia and conquered the Balkans. In 1453, Constantinople fell to an Ottoman army led by Sultan Mehmed II.

The Ottoman Empire reached its zenith during the reign of Süleyman the Magnificent (1522–66). During this period the empire stretched from the gates of Vienna to the tips of the Arabian Peninsula. The Ottoman navies were so invincible that they turned the Mediterranean into a Turkish sea.

Turkish warrior

After Süleyman's death, the empire began its slow decline. The Peace of Carlowitz (1699), with its loss of territories, marked the beginning of the end. The next blow came with the Treaty of Küçük Kaynarca (1774) signed with Russia, which was now consolidated under the House of Romanov. Soon afterwards the Russians opened the Black Sea to commerce and navigation. Within a decade, Crimea and Caucasia were under Russian rule. Tsarist Russia and the Ottoman Empire fought 17 wars.

In the early 20th century the empire was plunged into one war after another, culminating with its defeat in World War I, during which it had sided with Germany and Austria-Hungary. It was quickly carved up among the victors. Istanbul was occupied by the British, while the Italians seized Bodrum, Marmaris, Antalya and the southwest coast. The French occupied the Cilician coast.

In May 1919, the Greek army invaded Izmir. Three days later Mustafa Kemal Pasha (later named Atatürk), the victorious commander of the Turkish forces at Gallipoli, arrived at the northeast Black Sea port of Samsun and began the three-year national struggle for independence. Under Atatürk Turkish nationalism was ignited, the Greek army was defeated and the French were pushed back. Italy withdrew its troops, and the allied powers signed an armistice in 1922. The Treaty of Lausanne (1923) recognised Turkey's present boundaries, ended the capitulations and allowed for the exchange of minorities between Greece and Turkey.

Turkey was proclaimed a republic on 28 October 1923, and Kemal Atatürk was elected its first president with Ankara designated as the capital. Sweeping reforms were carried out by Atatürk to westernise the nation. The sultanate was abolished and the caliphate suppressed. The founding fathers of the state replaced the Sharia, the Islamic Holy law, with civil, trade and criminal codes adopted from the West. In 1925, the fez, a symbol of Islamic Orthodoxy, was banned and replaced by the *şapka*, a Western-style hat with a brim, and in 1928, the Latin alphabet replaced the Ottoman script. Women, who had been treated as second-class citizens under the Ottomans, were encouraged to enter the civil service and were granted suffrage. Eighteen women were elected deputies in 1936.

During this period the Turkish Coast was largely ignored. The potential for tourism wasn't realised until the early 1980s, quite late compared with elsewhere on the Mediterranean. When it came, however, it was explosive. Since then the region has hardly looked back, at least not from an economic point of view. Small fishing villages have expanded into large towns, with well-equipped marinas and long tentacles of hotels and apartment complexes. In summer migrant workers pour in from the poor hinterland.

But this affluent region is not immune to the problems that rack the rest of Turkey. In June 1994, for example, the PKK (Kurdistan Workers Party) claimed responsibility for a spate of bomb attacks on the popular resorts of Fethiye and Marmaris. In bringing its conflict to the Turkish Coast the PKK's purpose was two-fold: to bring their struggle for self-determination to the sudden attention of the world's media and to damage the Turkish economy.

Turkish beaches pull the crowds

Historical Highlights

Old Stone Age (600,000 BC): Cave-dwellings at Karain, Beldibi and Belbaşi, near Antalya.

2000–1200 BC Hittites establish capital at Hattush and extend rule over central and western Anatolia; first written history.

1100–1200 Aeolian and Ionian Greek migrants establish settlements along the Aegean Coast.

900 Rise of the Carians, Lycians and Phrygians.

800 Foundation of the Panionic League; rise of Ionian Aeolian Greek culture in Western Anatolia.

700 Rise of the Lydians.

650 Cimmerians destroy most cities in western Anatolia.

561–546 Reign of King Croesus of Lydia.

546 King Cyrus of Persia defeats Croesus, beginning Persian domination of western Anatolia.

499 Ionian cities revolt against Persian rule. The rebellion is crushed.

386 Persia subjugates Ionia again.

334 Alexander the Great invades western Anatolia in his campaign of empire building.

133 Attalus III, the king of Pergamum, bequeaths his kingdom to Rome.

AD 44–56 St Paul journeys through southern and western Anatolia to spread teachings of Jesus.

330 Constantine establishes Constantinople as the new capital of the Roman Empire.

677–718 Arab armies sweep across southern and western Anatolia, wreaking destruction in their path, but fail to conquer Constantinople.

1071 Seljuk Turks defeat Byzantines at the Battle of Manzikert and overrun most of Anatolia.

1096 First Crusade of Latin armies invade western and southern Anatolia on their way to Jerusalem.

1240 Ottoman Turks descend on western Anatolia as vassals of the Seljuk dynasty.

1242 The Seljuks are defeated by Mongols, ending their domination of Anatolia.

1451 The Ottomans, under Mehmet II, capture Constantinople; the city is renamed Istanbul; the Ottoman capital is established there.

1520–66 Reign of Süleyman the Magnificent. Height of Ottoman power; Ottomans conquer Rhodes, Baghdad, Hungary and Libya.

1699 The Treaty of Carlowitz marks the first Ottoman defeat. The Ottomans lose many central European territories.

1914 Turkey joins World War I as ally of Germany. Russia, France and Britain declare war on Turkey.

1918 Turks are defeated in World War I.

1919 Allied forces occupy Istanbul and the coastal areas of Turkey as part of World War I spoils. Italian troops occupy Antalya and southwest Turkey. The Greek army occupies Izmir and invades western Anatolia.

1919–22 Turkish War of Independence. Greeks are defeated by the Turks and leave Anatolia. Other allied powers also withdraw.

1923 Treaty of Lausanne establishes sovereignty of modern Turkey, determines borders, and organises the exchange of minorities between Greece and Turkey; Turkish Republic is declared; the sultanate and the caliphate are abolished; Kemal Atatürk becomes first president.

1925–38 Series of westernising economic and social reforms are introduced by Atatürk.

1925 Author Cevat Şatir Kabaagaçli is exiled to Bodrum. Through his writings, he popularises the Turkish Coast.

1982 A 14th-century BC shipwreck, the oldest known in the world, is discovered by sponge divers off Kaş. The find sheds light on sophisticated Bronze Age trade in the Eastern Mediterranean.

1984–present Hotel construction boom takes place along the Turkish Coast, and the region rapidly becomes a major international travel destination.

South West Turkey

25 miles/ 40 km

Bodrum

The most international of Turkey's cities, Bodrum is renowned for its foreign restaurants, party-town atmosphere and bohemian lifestyle. This combination is especially appealing to young foreigners and Western-oriented Turks, who flock here in summer to swim and sun themselves on the many beaches by day and gather at its many outdoor pubs, discos and bars to drink, dance and party all night. 'Bodrum,' local denizens are fond of saying, 'is 30 percent sex, 25 percent love and 45 percent relaxation.'

In ancient times the city was known as Halicarnassus, ruled by a Carian dynasty. Alexander the Great arrived in Halicarnassus in 334BC. and conquered the city. After his death the city continued as a Graeco-Roman city until 654AD when it was completely destroyed by the Arab invasions of Anatolia, and wiped from the pages of history until the 15th century. The Knights of St John, revived the city in 1402, when they were given possession of Halicarnassus by Tamerlane, the oriental despot whose armies swept through Anatolia. The Knights built the Castle of St Peter, after their patron saint, and named their city Petronium, from which the modern Turkish name Bodrum is derived. The Knights finally abandoned the city in 1522 when the Ottoman sultan Süleyman the Magnificent conquered Rhodes, their stronghold.

Bodrum is a small town – you can walk from one end to the other in about 45 minutes – and its few archaeological sights can be visited in a few hours; but it makes a lively base for taking excursions into the countryside or boat trips to nearby bays and villages.

View of Bodrum harbour

1. In and Around Bodrum

Visit the Castle of St Peter; ride a camel along the quay; lunch at the harbour; walk to the ruins of the Mausoleum of Halicarnassus and the amphitheatre; then take a taxi to Gümbet for swimming and windsurfing.

After breakfast, leave your hotel around 9.30am and set off for Bodrum Castle, better known as the **Castle of St Peter.** Allow for a two-hour tour of the castle itself and its Museum of Underwater Archaeology (it closes for lunch noon–3pm in summer and noon–1pm in winter). Built between 1402 and 1503 by the Knights of St John, an international Catholic monastic order, also known as the Knights Hospitalers of St John of Jerusalem, the Knights of Rhodes and later as the Knights of Malta, the castle was used as a base for raids on the Aegean Coast, and served as a refuge for Christians fleeing Turkish captivity. The Knights kept a special breed of dog, simi-

Castle of St Peter

lar to the St Bernard, which could identify Christian fugitives and lead them to the castle.

The Knights, whose members comprised noblemen of eight different countries, held the castle from 1402–1522. When Rhodes, their headquarters in the eastern Mediterranean, fell to the Ottoman Turks they were obliged to withdraw to Malta.

To build the castle, the Knights used green stones, statuary, masonry and marble slabs from the nearby Mausoleum of Halicarnas-

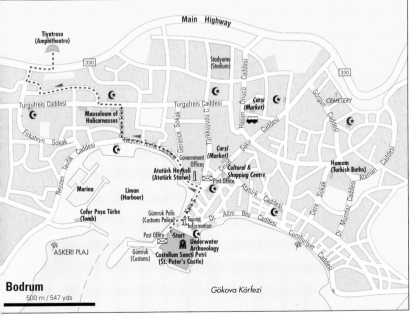

Bodrum
500 m / 547 yds

In the castle grounds

sus, which they found in ruins, apparently destroyed by an earthquake sometime after the 12th century. In 1844, British archaeologists removed some of the marble slabs from the mausoleum to the British Museum. Among these slabs were ones showing the *Amazonomachy*, a battle between the Greeks and the Amazons.

The castle was used in various ways by the Turks. It served as a military base during the 1824 Greek uprising and was later converted into a dungeon for political offenders.

Enter the castle through a gate along the harbour, paying a small admission fee at the front booth, and walk up the covered stone ramp. Cross a small footbridge to the inner castle, then proceed through several gateways, on which the knights' coats of arms are displayed, to the courtyard and the **Museum of Underwater Archaeology**.

The museum is among the most impressive of its kind in the world. Opened in 1960, it contains the remains of the world's oldest known shipwrecks, discovered along the Turkish Coast by scientists of the Institute of Nautical Archaeology (INA). Founded in 1973 by George Bass, a renowned American underwater archaeologist, the INA has discovered and mapped more than 125 shipwrecks off the Turkish Coast, one of the richest shores for sunken ships in the world. About 10 percent of the museum's relics were found during excavations on land.

The building on the right upon entering the courtyard was once a Gothic chapel, which now houses a 7th-century Byzantine shipwreck and its cargo, discovered off the Turkish island Yassi Ada by George Bass and his divers. Since 1982, Bass and his team have been excavating the oldest known shipwreck, dating from the 14th century BC, discovered by a sponge diver off Uluburun, near Kaş. Their finds included a gold pendant of an eagle, a Mycenian vase, amber beads of Baltic origin, an unworked ivory tusk, a lamb's head drinking cup, an amphora, a Canaanite sword, a gold chalice and hundreds of other items.

The courtyard is an open-air museum displaying amphora, pottery and statuary. A pleasant outdoor café occupies one corner. To its right is the **Shipwreck Hall** which contains the hull and cargo of an 11th-century shipwreck that was found at **Serçe Limanı,** a shallow cove 38km (24 miles) southwest of Marmaris. A series of steps behind the Bronze-Age Hall lead to the so-called Glass Wreck. This exhibition contains hundreds of coloured glass jars, bottles and vases, retrieved in 1977 from the Serçe Limanı wreck. The vessel was believed to have been transporting scrap glass from the Arab world to Constantinople when it ran aground and sank. Divers retrieved more than 2.5 tons (2,500kg) of scrap glass and semi-finished products from the bottom of the sea. The hall also displays a miniature model showing an underwater excavation of a shipwreck.

One feature of the castle often missed is its garden, which contains one of each of the species of trees and plants growing in the Mediterranean region, as well as pheasants, peacocks, ducks, geese and rabbits that roam freely.

Walk up the slope behind the Hall of the Glass Wreck and you come to the **Italian Tower**, which was the residence of the Italian Knights. Today it houses the **Coin and Jewellery Hall**, a collection spanning several centuries. Just behind the Italian Tower is a gallery containing the remains of a Carian princess, whose tomb was discovered during the construction of a building near Bodrum. In addition to the sarcophagus, skull and bones, archaeologists found a gold myrtle crown, bracelets and jewellery (on display). A replica of the princess, reconstructed by Manchester University physicians, can also be seen.

To the left of the Italian Tower is the **French Tower**, where the French Knights resided. The vaulted section linking the two towers was once the residence of the governor of the castle. Cross the northern moat and turn left. You have now come to the **English Tower**, at the farthest corner of the castle. On its walls are the coats of arms of Edward IV, one of the members of the House of Plantagenet, the dynasty which ruled England from 1154–1485, and of the captains of the Knights, Sir Thomas Sheffield and John Kendall. Follow the eastern walls of the castle and you come to the **Dungeon**, a tower where Muslim prisoners were kept and tortured. Above the inner door is an inscription in Latin: INDE DEUS ABEST, meaning 'God does not exist in this place.'

Above the dungeon is the **Mass Burial Grave of Galley Slaves** which includes the bones of 13 galley slaves tortured to death.

Inside the **German Tower**, are banners of Germanic tribes and the heads and antlers of antelopes. The tower is now used as a coffee-house. To its left, overlooking the isthmus and downtown Bodrum, is the **Snake Tower**, whose name is derived from a frieze in the form of a snake taken from the mausoleum and symbolising the serpent shape that Zeus, the supreme deity of the ancient Greeks, took before adopting human form. The tower is used to store amphora and is closed to the public. Nearby is a mosaic of the Roman era. Return to the lower courtyard and leave the castle.

At the harbour below the castle you can take a camel ride (lasting about 10 minutes).

Your transport awaits

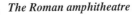

The Roman amphitheatre

Each animal, weighing nearly 1,000kg (1 ton), can carry up to four people at one time. Every gyrating step is an exhilarating experience for a person riding for the first time, and is a special treat for youngsters. After the camel ride, enjoy a leisurely lunch on the quayside with a view of the yachts. Try some *meze* appetisers, such as *ahtapot salata* (tender octopus lightly cooked and steeped in olive oil and lemon juice, served with green salad and tomatoes).

After lunch, take a walk along Neyzen Tevfik Caddesi, to the site of the Mausoleum of Halicarnassus. The semicircular street running along the harbour is named after Neyzen Tevfik Kolaylı (1879–1953), a Turkish poet famous for satirical verses. Born and raised in Bodrum, where his father taught, Tevfik was also a virtuoso of the *ney* (Turkish flute), from which he got his name.

Turn right at Hamam Sokak after passing the mosque, walk uphill and turn left at Turgutreis Caddesi. The **Mausoleum of Halicarnassus** (small admission charge) is located 100 metres/yards away on the left-hand side of the street, hidden by a wall. A 20-minute stay should suffice.

What remains of the mausoleum – the foundation, a jumble of masonry and tumbled columns – belies its original status as one of the Seven Wonders of the Ancient World. The structure, built in the 4th century BC by Queen Artemesia as the imposing tomb of her husband and brother, King Mausolus, originally consisted of a high base, a peristyle of 36 columns, a pyramid of 24 steps, crowned by a quadriga, a four-horsed chariot. The monument, a small model of which can be seen in the enclosed area, was 42 metres (138ft) in height and 36 sq m (400 sq ft) in area. A Danish expedition led by Kristian Jeppesen in the 1970s uncovered a few new slabs and friezes depicting the battle between Greeks and Amazons, now in the enclosure.

The Knights of St John, seeking building material for their castle, pillaged and destroyed the remains of the mausoleum in the 15th century. British archaeologists Lord Stratford and C T Newton, who excavated the site separately in the mid-19th century, uncovered reliefs and the colossal statues of Mausolus and Artemesia, now in the British Museum.

A short walk uphill along one of the narrow streets from the mausoleum will bring you to the Roman amphitheatre, located on the other side of the Bodrum–Izmir Road, overlooking the town. Spend a few minutes admiring the view of Bodrum's castle and harbour before returning to your hotel.

For an afternoon of beach pursuits, take a taxi to **Gümbet**, a village with a long sandy beach, about 5km (3 miles) from Bodrum

Beach encounter

(alternatively you can share a jeep: these run between Gümbet and Bodrum, leaving every 10 minutes from the Bodrum bus station off Cevat Şakir Caddesi). Gümbet means water cistern, named after the white domed water collectors in the surrounding hills.

Since windsurfing was introduced in the early 1980s, Gümbet has acquired a good reputation among professional windsurfers. Its surrounding hills and long, deep bay protect surfers from dangerous offshore winds. Its winters are mild, allowing windsurfing even as late as December.

Equipment can be hired at Hotel Ayaz, Hotel Park Palas and Hotel Sami. In addition to windsurfing, all three offer water skiing, banana boat riding, canoeing, parasailing, and sea biking. The beach is also excellent for simply swimming and tanning.

After swimming at Gümbet, return to Bodrum for dinner, stopping off for a few minutes at the **Cemetery of Cevat Şakir Kabaağaçlı** (1890–1973), a Bohemian British-educated author knowns as the 'Fisherman of Halicarnassus'. Exiled to Bodrum in 1925 for his unorthodox political views, Kabaağaçlı popularised the town with his writings, attracting like-minded intellectuals. Overlooking Bodrum from a hill, the plain tomb is as unpretentious as the man was who lies inside it. Beside the grave are the words: 'Balıkçı merhaba' ('Fisherman, hello'), the author's favourite expression. Kabaağaçlı lived in Bodrum nearly 25 years.

After a rest at your hotel, spend some time walking through downtown Bodrum, along Kale Sokak, Dr Alim Bey Caddesi and Cumhuriyet Caddesi, good streets for shopping. The downtown area is closed to vehicles between dawn and midnight. Don't be surprised if you run into international celebrities, such as pop star Phil Collins, actress Barbra Streisand, Prince Charles or actor Michael Douglas, who frequently visit Bodrum as guests of Ahmet Ertegün, the Turco-American businessman who owns Atlantic Records. Ertegün bought a house here in the late 1970s.

You can buy handwoven wool Milâs carpets at **Mehmet Çengel** (Çarşı Mahalesi Belediye Meydanı) and at **Asian Carpets and Kilims** (Dr Alim Bey Bedesteni, Cumhuriyet Caddesi). A good range

of handmade leather sandals, shoes, slippers, belts and bags can be purchased at **Yaban Sandalet Matsan Ticaret** (Cumhuriyet Caddesi, 39). One of Bodrum's few remaining sandalmakers is Şerafettin Özbaş, who runs **Şeref Sandalet** (Cumhuriyet Caddesi, 168).

How about a hat?

You can watch him making the sandals in his shop. Leather jackets and sheepskin coats from Istanbul are sold at **Centrum Leather** (Cumhuriyet Caddesi, Dr Alim Bey Bedesteni) and at **Kontes** (Cumhuriyet Caddesi, 50) and in scores of other shops. Also worth buying are bath sponges, a speciality of Bodrum, sold on the streets by peddlers. Turkey is the world's leading producer of natural sea sponges, and Bodrum is the capital of the nation's sponge-diving industry.

By now you may be hungry. **Kortan Restaurant** (Cumhuriyet Caddesi, 32) is a convivial place for dinner. Owned by Istanbul businessman Ali Günaydın and his son Zeki, it occupies an old Bodrum house and specialises in grilled meats and fish. Afterwards sample Bodrum's nightlife. Beware the sign '*Damsız Girilmez*' at the entrance of some discos and bars: this means a man must be accompanied by a woman. One other caveat: prices for drinks vary considerably from bar to bar, especially if there is live music. Don't be shocked if you end up paying three times more for a fruit cocktail at one bar than you did at the disco next door.

Start out at the upmarket and immensely popular **Halikarnas Bar and Nightclub** (Cumhuriyet Caddesi, 178). Its outdoor, seaside disco resembles a Greek acropolis with an odeon and an amphitheatre. The huge dance floor can hold several hundred people at once.

Afterwards move on to **Sensi Bar** (Cumhuriyet Caddesi, 143), a

two-storey, open-air bar with a terrace overlooking the busy street. For those who prefer folk music, **Beyaz Ev** (the White House) next door may be the best bet in town. Here you can listen to Turkish musicians playing the electric guitar and singing popular blues and rock tunes.

Meanwhile **Rick's Bar** (Cumhuriyet Caddesi, 134) appeals to young British tourists and you can listen to the pop-

Darkness falls on Bodrum

ular pop singers at **Big Ben Bar** (Cumhuriyet Caddesi), along the seashore. The crowded **Yetigari** (Dr Alim Bey Caddesi, 36) and the **Hadi Gari Cafe Bar** next door should top off your night. The Hadi Gari has the reputation of being the best bar in Turkey. Try some of the drinks it's famous for, such as Hadi Gari Winds, a mixture of grenadine and Gordon's Gin with fruit juices. If you can't find a place in Hadi Gari, try Kavalye Bar on the same street for a night of pop music by candlelight.

2. A Drive to Milâs

A day in the country near Bodrum, beginning with Beçin Kale, a medieval stronghold; then to Milâs, visiting the Gümüşkesen Mausoleum; continue to Labraynda, a Carian religious centre; see the world's only carpet farm; drive to Gümüşlük; visit the Myndos ruins and sunken city.

For this tour of the country around Milâs, 65km/40 miles north of Bodrum (an hour's drive), you should hire a car. There are numerous car hire firms in Bodrum, most on Neyzen Tevfik Caddesi.

The drive to Milâs, along the Bodrum–Izmir highway is a smooth ride over rolling hills and following the shoreline to **Güvercinlik**, a resort village with a long, deep bay. From there, it cuts inland, passing orchards, olive groves and cotton fields. As you near Milâs, look out for the Ildız Carpet Farm on your left. You will return to this in the afternoon.

Before entering Milâs, stop off at **Beçin Kale**, a ruined 14th-century stronghold, standing on top of a flat rocky hill 3km (2 miles) out of town. A dirt road near the junction of the Bodrum–Izmir and Milâs–Muğla roads leads to the site.

Just inside the gates, on the right, is a flight of solid marble steps, believed to be part of an ancient temple. Nearby is the interesting **Medrese of Ahmet Gazi**, an Islamic religious school named after a Menteseoglu statesman, Ahmet Gazi. He and his wife are buried next to each other in an open part of the *medrese*, and are considered saints by the local inhabitants. Local pilgrims visit the tombs and put shreds of cloth on the headstones so that their wishes may be granted.

Behind the *medrese* are the ruins of a mosque. Admire the striking view of Milâs and the valley below. You can buy soft drinks from a small stand. Pottery shards found around Beçin Kale dating from the 4th and 7th centuries BC have led the British archaeologist J M Cook to suggest that this was the original site of the ancient city of Mylasa – a theory supported by the fact that the Carians built their cities on high ground, for defence purposes.

Milâs, today one of Turkey's leading producers of handmade wool carpets, lies to the left of the highway. This market town, known to the ancients as Mylasa, was once the capital of the Carian state, but was ruled successively by the Persians, Alexander the Great, the Romans, the Byzantines and now the Turks.

The most impressive monument in Milâs is the Roman mausoleum known as **Gümüşkesen** ('silver purse'), visible from every point in town. Located in a public park over-

Milâs from the hills

Gateway to Milâs

looking Milâs, the monument is a smaller replica of the Mausoleum of Halicarnassus, with a pyramidal roof supported by columns. It was built in the 1st century AD, and gets its Turkish name from alleged treasures hidden inside its crypt, which was long ago broken into but is now locked. A strange hole exists on the floor of the funerary monument surmounting the sepulchral chamber below. This hole was used by the family of the deceased to pour milk, honey and wine into the chamber to feed the spirit of their loved one.

The ruins of a Roman temple can be seen near the **Belediye Binası**, the town hall, but all that remains is a fluted column on an elevated marble floor.

Now drive into the centre of Milâs and stop off at its colourful market place (Pazar Yeri) to pick up bread, cheese, grapes, etc, for a picnic in the Carian religious centre of Labraynda. Before going to Labraynda, however, visit the **Tomb of Güveç Dede**, a minor Islamic saint, in the **Hacı Ilyas District** of the town. Also stroll to the two 14th-century Turkish mosques nearby and the more impressive **Firuz Bey Camii** (1397), also known as the **Gök Camii**, with its pinkish marble facade.

One other sight not be missed in Milâs is the **Baltalı Kapı**, or the 'Gate of the Axe', on the main street, just beside the state hospital (Devlet Hastanesi). Baltalı Kapı derives its name from the frieze of a double axe on its facade, symbolising the divine Kingdom of Caria. The arched gate was, in ancient times, the beginning of the paved 13-km (8-mile) 'Sacred Way' connecting Milâs with the holy shrine of Labraynda in the hills. Traces of this holy road can still be seen.

Labraynda, 700 metres (2,300ft) above sea level, is situated along a bumpy and winding dirt road off the Milâs–Izmir Highway, 13km

The Temple of Zeus

(8 miles) from Milâs (the turn is about 3km/2 miles out of town). Built on terraces, it dates back to the 4th century BC. Its most important site is the **Temple of Zeus, Labrayndus**, the god of the double axe and the patron deity of Caria, which is located on an upper terrace. Behind the temple is the **First Andron**, a well-preserved building with a 2-metre- (6-ft-) thick wall. The **Androns** — there are several at the site — were where priests of the shrine gathered for social purposes. Next to it was a residence for the clergy. Also of interest is a large **tomb**, with three sarcophagi inside, found on the slope overlooking the temple.

Mausolus and other Carian kings maintained at Labraynda a **Summer Palace**, which has not yet been excavated, but is believed to lie near the temple. The holy community also had a **Sacred Pool of Oracle Fish** adorned with earrings and necklaces. Some early chronicles argued that these fish were capable of making yes-and-no prophecies by accepting or rejecting food offered after a question. The pool was located in the building today marked as the **Ablution Hall**, along a wall at the lower terrace.

Return to your car and have a picnic at the tiny coffeehouse by the road before leaving the hamlet. Tea is served in pretty tulip-shaped glasses.

Now drive to the world's only carpet farm, the **Ildız Carpet Farm**, on the Bodrum–Milâs Highway (10km/6 miles) out of Milâs. Here, experts wash and dry handmade wool carpets manufactured or bought by the Ildız Company, one of Turkey's leading carpet producers and exporters. The firm specialises in the manufacture of pastel-coloured wool carpets, using natural root dyes. The 7-ha (17-acre) farm dries as many as 20,000 carpets at one time. If you visit the farm in early summer, you will see thousands of carpets spread out like a huge colourful mosaic.

After weaving, the backsides of the carpets are burned until they become charcoal black. They are then washed with a special shampoo and vinegar, dried in a gigantic centrifuge, and spread out under the sun for as long as three months, after which they are categorised according to the degree of colour fading (there are five classes), and priced. Carpets whose colours have faded (those coloured with artificial dyes) sell at lower prices.

Ildız, which operates the **Tribal Art** chain of carpet stores in Turkey, opened the farm in 1984 to revive carpet-making in Milâs, a traditional carpet weaving centre. The farm is located in a dry, almost rain-free region. Its beautiful guest house, where foreign carpet buyers can stay while inspecting orders, is a copy of a Turkish house and won the Aga Khan Award for Architecture in 1983.

Leave the carpet farm and drive to **Gümüşlük**, about 80km (50

Geometric detail

miles) away, at the western tip of the Bodrum Peninsula, to explore the ruins of the ancient city of **Myndos** and have dinner at a seaside fish restaurant. Gümüşlük, or 'silver coin', is built in two well sheltered bays. A peninsula on the northwest protects it from the *meltem*, the brisk summer wind that pounds Turkey's Aegean Coast, making it a favourite stopover for yachtsmen sailing between Bodrum and Izmir.

Tavşan Ada (Rabbit Island) divides the bays – its name derives from a colony of rabbits raised by the locals on the island to sell at market. Gümüşlük has several makeshift piers where smaller boats can anchor. Boat tours leave every Tuesday, Thursday, Saturday and Sunday at 11am during the summer for nearby coves, one of which includes the **Sunken City**, where you can see the remains of what were probably parts of old Myndos (the last boat returns at 7.30pm). Myndos was a settlement of the Lelegians, a seafaring people related to the Carians. The Carian King Mausolus moved most of the people living in Myndos and other neighbouring towns to Halicarnassus in the 4th century BC to create a thriving capital.

Return to the village to view the stunning sunset and enjoy a fish supper: *barbunya* (striped mullet) best served fried, or *karagöz* (white sea bream) which is usually grilled. To start with, try some local *meze* dishes such as *semizotu salatası*, a purslane salad prepared with yoghurt, garlic, red peppers and olive oil, and *mercimek piyazı*, lentil salad with onions, dill, vinegar, sugar, olive oil and salt. After dinner, return to Bodrum.

3. Boat Trip around Bodrum Peninsula

A boat trip to Karaada and nearby beaches for swimming. Boats for this day trip leave Bodrum harbour at 11am sharp.

These motor-driven boats, usually Bodrum-built caïques, are capable of taking 30 people at one time.

Karaada is the dark island that guards Bodrum's bay. It takes about 25 minutes to get to Karaada, which is famous for its mud baths next to the shore. 'These baths', Kabaağaçlı, the Fisherman of Halicarnassus once wrote, 'are nearly capable of resurrecting the dead.' You have half an hour to wade ashore and try a mud bath, or to swim in the clear blue waters. Then return to your boat for a one-hour trip to Ortakent Beach. The tract of land you see on your

left is the Greek island of Kos.

On the way to Ortakent Beach, the boat passes through **Ada Boğazı**, a shallow body of water separating a minuscule island, **Iç Ada**, from the Bodrum

Choose your transport

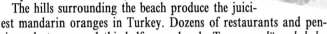

Grab a kebab

Peninsula and often referred to as the 'Aquarium' because of the wealth of marine life found at its sandy bottom. After passing **Çelebi Island** it arrives at **Ortakent Beach**, where it stops for lunch (not included in the price of the boat ride).

The hills surrounding the beach produce the juiciest mandarin oranges in Turkey. Dozens of restaurants and pensions cluster around this half-moon beach. Try some *döner kebabı*, tender slices of beef prepared on a revolving spit and served on *pide* bread with tomato sauce and yoghurt, at one of the beach restaurants.

After the meal, you have about 30 minutes before your boat heads back to Bodrum, which is just long enough for a quick dip or to try an exhilarating banana boat ride.

On the return voyage to Bodrum, you will pass two promontories on which stand the Aktur Holiday Villas. These houses are owned by prominent Turks, including the family of the late President Turgut Özal. The next wide bay is Bitez, one of Bodrum's most popular resorts.

The captain will pilot the boat back to Ada Boğazı for a 45-minute stop, allowing a swim in one of the deserted coves. If you swim ashore, make sure you don't step on any spiny sea urchins whose painful stings can ruin your holiday. The captain will sideskirt Gümbet Bay, with its windsurfers, and then skim past the luxurious five-star Club M Holiday Village and Hotel to enter **Bardakçı**, the last cove before Bodrum, which has a fine sandy beach.

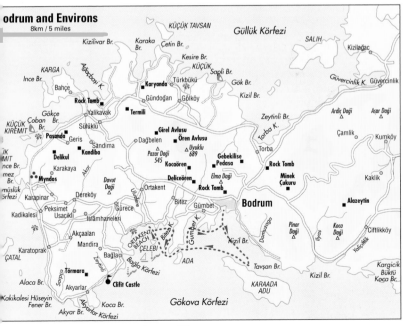

Bodrum and Environs
8km / 5 miles

Water babies

According to legend, it was at Bardakçı that Hermaphrodite, the son of Hermes and Aphrodite, fell in love with the nymph Salmacis, with whom he was united in one body, with both male and female sexual characteristics. The cove lives up to its reputation for sexual diversity even today. It was the favourite beach of Zeki Müren, a popular transvestite singer who made Bodrum his home. Bardakçı is often referred to as the **Cove of the Pasha**, a nickname for Müren, who died in 1996.

The boat arrives back in Bodrum harbour around 6.30pm.

My suggestion for dinner this evening is **Han Restaurant** on Kale Sokak. Converted from a caravanserai, Han is a lively place with Turkish music, folklore performances and belly dancing. It is not unusual for customers to take to the dance floor and do the *çifteteli*, a kind of belly dance. The meal includes a rich array of *meze* dishes, fish, meats and pastries.

For more reserved visitors who don't care to participate in floor shows, **Amphora Restaurant** by the marina on Neyzen Teufik Caddesi offers quality Turkish cuisine in a 200-year-old house with restful views of gently swaying yachts.

4. Ephesus

A drive through the countryside to Ephesus, one of the great cities of antiquity, stopping off at the Temple of Euromos. In the afternoon, visit the Great Temple of Artemis, the castle of Selçuk and the church of St John, Isa Bey Mosque, and drive to the House of the Virgin Mary. Dinner is in Kuşadası, from where you can return to Bodrum or spend the night.

As Ephesus is about 180km (112 miles) from Bodrum, near the town of Selçuk, off the Bodrum-Izmir Highway, and takes about two hours by car, leave very early. You will have a full-day's programme of sight-seeing.

After Milâs, the road passes through the rugged Carian Hills. About 13km (8 miles) from Milâs, towards Izmir, the columns of a temple rise close to the road. This temple was part of **Euromos**, one of the three largest cities of the Carian state. Stop for a few minutes to inspect this amazing temple, one of the best preserved

in Anatolia. Sixteen of its columns are still standing. Other sites in the city include a badly ruined amphitheatre, an agora and some tomb chambers.

After another 24km (15 miles), you come to **Lake Bafa** (Bafa Gölü), once part of the Aegean Sea. The silting of the Büyük Menderes River (the Mean-

Weighing cotton

der) has left it landlocked 20km (12 miles) from the sea. You might want to have tea at one of the lakeside coffeehouses facing the **Beş Parmak Dağı** (Mt Latmus of the Ancients) before continuing.

North of Lake Bafa stretch the immense, marshy flatlands that make up the **Büyük Menderes River Valley**, one of Turkey's leading cotton-producing areas. The many twists and turns in the 584-km (365-mile) Büyük Menderes coined the English verb 'to meander'.

After the cotton boom town of **Söke** on your left, you soon reach hills and enter the town of **Selçuk**, a small but flourishing tourist centre with a castle, located about 2km (1 mile) from Ephesus. Before touring the ruins, visit Selçuk's **Ephesus Museum** (8.30am–noon and 1–6pm), which has one of the finest collections of antiquities in the world. Housing friezes and statues unearthed in Ephesus, it includes the cult statues of the Anatolian fertility goddess Artemis (known as Diana to the Romans). The two statues of Artemis on display emphasise the importance this great mother goddess once had. From the hips to the toes of both statues, flowers and bees are visible. The belt of the *Great Artemis* (the one

wearing the tall crown, displayed at the western end of the hall) also shows bees and flowers. Next to the *Beautiful Artemis* (displayed at the eastern end of the hall) is a headless statue of Artemis with bees and flowers on her chest. Both statues are many breasted: breasts, bees and flowers were symbols of fertility, clearly showing the Ionic dependence on nature.

Other notable artifacts include the bust of Alexander's general Lysimachus,

The Colonnaded Street in Ephesus

and various statues of Roman emperors and senators. The tiny statue of Eros on a dolphin and the miniature bronze statues of Priapus, a fertility god whose phallus was equal to its height, also adorn the museum's hall. The statue was found in the brothel of Ephesus. Priapus, also known as the God Bes, ranked high among the ancient Anatolian gods, and was widely worshipped by early Anatolian women seeking marriage and children.

Now drive on to **Ephesus**. In the 2nd century AD, Ephesus was a flourishing Aegean port with more than 250,000 inhabitants and known as the 'first and greatest metropolis of Asia'. Its eventual decline was due to the accumulation of silt at the mouth of the Kaystros (the Küçük Menderes) river, which ruined its harbour. Today, it lies 5km (3 miles) inland. It is one of Turkey's most popular destinations, attracting more than 2 million tourists annually.

Relief detail

Over the centuries, Ephesus was home to many civilisations and religions. Little is known about its earliest inhabitants, but from Mycenean bowls discovered by archaeologists it is believed that a Carian settlement may have existed on the site of the present ruins as early at 1400BC.

Ephesus was colonised by 1000BC, by Ionian Greek settlers from Athens, led by Androklos, the son of an Athenian king. His descendants ruled the city for the next four centuries. The Ionians introduced the cult of Artemis, their patron goddess, and built great shrines for the deity.

In 560BC, the Lydian king Croesus captured Ephesus, and ruled for less than 14 years. By the end of his reign, Ephesus had become western Asia Minor's most affluent city. After the Persian King Cyrus defeated Croesus in 546BC, the city became a Persian satraphy, or province. Between 546–334BC, the Ionian region was in turmoil as Greeks and Persians fought each other. When Alexander the Great defeated the Persians at the Battle of the Granicus in 334BC, Ephesus was liberated and it became semi-democratic.

Lysimachus, one of Alexander's lesser generals, ruled the city. It was later briefly dominated by the Ptolemites of Egypt before being annexed by the Attalid kings of Pergamum in 188BC.

Roman control of Ephesus began after 133BC after the last Attalid king bequeathed his territories to Rome. In 27BC the Roman Emperor Augustus proclaimed Ephesus capital of the Asian province. It was during this period that Ephesus became one of the largest cities in the Roman Empire and one of only three cities to have street lighting. Most of the buildings visible today date from the Roman era.

Following a devastating attack by a large Gothic fleet in AD262, ancient Ephesus began to decline as a major trading centre.

Previous to this its large community of Gentiles and Jews had become a target of the proselytising activities of St Paul. City silversmiths, whose trade in cult objects was harmed by St Paul's condemnation of idols, rioted against the Christian converts. During one of these disturbances, the opponents to the Christians jammed the Ephesus theatre chanting: 'Great is Artemis of the Ephesians!'

During this era, Christians were persecuted for refusing to make animal sacrifices and worship the pagan gods. They were crucified, murdered in the streets, and fed to lions in Ephesus Stadium to entertain Roman crowds of up to 70,000 people.

St Paul was driven from Ephesus, only to be martyred in Rome, but Christianity gained a permanent foothold. Ephesus became one of the earliest Christian communities in the Eastern Mediterranean and is mentioned as one of the Seven Churches in the New Testament's Book of Revelations. Both the Virgin Mary and the Apostle St John, who fled persecutions in Jerusalem, are believed to have lived and died here.

In the 4th century, when Christianity became the official religion to Rome, all the seats in Ephesus Stadium where Christians had been tortured to death were destroyed. Today the stadium is the scene for a camel wrestling festival held every January, and the Izmir International Music Festival every summer.

By the 4th century, the magnificence of Ephesus had dwindled, its harbour silted up. When the Seljuk Turks arrived in 1304 all that remained was a dusty Byzantine village which was easily overrun. The Ottoman Turks conquered the city in 1426.

When the travel writer H.V. Morton visited the site in the mid-1930s he found it 'with no sign of life but a goatherd leaning on a broken sarcophagus or a lonely peasant outlined against a mournful sunset. Few people ever visit it. Ephesus has a weird, haunted look.' The late George Bean, who attempted to locate the site in 1939, drove his vehicle along dirt roads and got lost in a cornfield.

Upon entering the ancient city from the Selçuk–Kuşadası road gate, the first building on your left is the **Vedius Gymnasium**, one of the best preserved buildings in Ephesus, built in AD150 as a combined gymnasium and bath-house complex. Next to it is the **Stadium**, where gladiatorial fights took place and Christians were tortured in Roman times.

Further up, on the right, are the remains of the **Church of the Virgin Mary**, the first church ever dedicated to the Virgin Mary. It was here that the Third Ecumenical Council proclaimed in AD431 that Mary was the mother of Jesus. This council recorded that Mary lived and died near Ephesus, and branded Nestor, Patriarch of Constantinople, a heretic for his denial of the virgin birth.

Next to the church stands the **Theatre Gymnasium,** with the **Harbour Gymnasium** and, behind it, the **Baths**.

A colonnaded street, the **Arcadian Way**, leads west to the ancient harbour. In the Roman era this street was lined with lamps.

The Arcadian Way and the amphitheatre

The **Ephesus Amphitheatre**, with a seating capacity of 24,000, is well preserved and used even today for international folklore performances and live concerts. It was here that the anti-Christian demonstrations instigated by the silversmiths took place. The theatre has superb acoustics. Even from the top row of seats, you can easily hear conversations on the orchestra floor far below.

ΕΠΙΣΤΗΜΗ
ΚΕΛΣΟΥ

Nearby is the **Agora**, or central shopping centre, and the **Celsus Library**. When Tiberius Julius Celsus, a famous Roman administrator, died in AD114, his son commissioned its library as a monument and mausoleum. Celsus was found buried inside a richly decorated marble sarcophagus under a library wall. The library was one of the largest in the ancient world, competing with those in Alexandria and Pergamum, and its spacious interior housed nearly 12,000 scrolls.

Next to it are the remains of the **Monumental Archway**, which resembles Hadrian's Gate in Athens.

Across the library are ruins of the **brothel**, indicating that institutionalised prostitution was practised in Ephesus. The upper storey of the house has been destroyed and only traces of frescoes remain.

The Agora

A mosaic in the dining room depicts the four seasons while a simple mosaic in the adjacent pool shows three maidens, a servant, a mouse eating crumbs, and a cat.

The so-called **Scholastica Baths** are next door, on **Curetes Street**, which runs on a northeast–southwest axis through the southern part of the ruins. Built in the 1st century, these heated baths were repaired frequently until about AD400. The **Statue of Christian Scholasticia**, the last notable to restore the baths, stands inside. As in all Roman baths, there were separate hot, tepid, and cold water rooms.

The **Temple of Hadrian**, completed in honour of Emperor Hadrian by AD138, stands in front of the Scholastica Baths. Behind the bases of four columns which once held statues of four Roman emperors rise four Corinthian columns. The ancient Romans, deified their emperors, dedicated temples to them and worshipped them like pagan gods. A decorated arch, featuring the face of Tyche, the goddess of fortune, crowns the temple's two central columns.

On the south side of Curetes Street, several stately houses built on the slopes of Bülbül Dağı (Nightingale Mountain) have been unearthed. These three-storey structures had courtyards, running water, heating, mosaic floors, and walls adorned with frescoes. Originally constructed during the reign of Augustus, these houses were frequently altered right up until the end of the 7th century. Two of them are restored and may be entered by climbing the steps just across the street from Hadrian's Temple. The 3rd-century BC **City Walls**, constructed by Lysimachus, run along the ridges of Bülbüldağ to the south and Panayırdağ to the north.

Other sites on the south side of the street include the remains of a pool-shaped structure that may have been a fountain, and an **octagonal tomb** with inscriptions, from the 1st century.

Curetes Street continues to a junction, where a road, described by archaeologists as **Domitian Street**, leads to the south, along the western end of the State Agora. Numerous monuments are situated near the junction, including the **Memmius Monument** built in the 1st century BC to honour Memmius, a Roman military commander and son of the dictator Sculla. The **Temple of Domitian**, dedicated to Emperor Domitian (AD81–96), is largely unrestored. To the east of the steps at the entrance to the Temple of Domitian stands a two-tiered column with reliefs. Just behind is the cool **Inscription Gallery** where numerous documents pertaining to the history of Ephesus have been found.

Return to the junction and turn east to the **State Agora**, where many municipal functions took place, such as meetings of the law courts. Located to the north of the State Agora is the **Prytaneion**, where the eternal flame of Ephesus burned and where the two famous statues of Artemis were found. Political business was conducted at the Prytaneion, the City Hall. Next to it is an edifice described as the **Basilica**, but about which little is known.

The **Temple of Serapis** (or Isis) is located at the southwestern corner of the Agora. The presence of this temple, dedicated to Serapis, the Egyptian god of the underworld and judge of the dead, is an indication of the city's close relations with Egypt. Eight massive marble columns, each weighing 27 tons, lie tumbled in front of the ruins.

The small theatre or **Odeon**, which is east of the Prytaneion and the basilica, seated 1,400 and was built in AD150. Although it was used for concerts, it was also the chamber for a 300-member governing body called the Boule.

Just next to the Odeon stands the mostly unexcavated **Varius Baths**. The western entrance to these baths is immediately across the **Latrina**, or public toilets. Hidden to the right of this entrance is a 50-cm (20-inch) tall relief of Artemis with an animal head facing right and holding a staff in her right hand. Ephesus ends at the **Magnesian Gates**, constructed by Emperor Vespasian (AD69–79)

Temple of Hadrian

and the only Ephesian gate to survive to the present times. The gate is linked by a sacred road to the Artemesion, or the Great Temple of Artemis, near the present city of Selçuk.

Return to the entrance of the ruins and have a spot of lunch at one of the busy restaurants which specialise in grilled meats.

After lunch, drive to the ruins of the **Temple of Artemis**, on the outskirts of Selçuk, on the road to Kuşadası. All that remains of the temple today is a single column standing in mud but it was once one of the Seven Wonders of the Ancient World (along with the Pyramids of Egypt; the Colossus of Rhodes; the Statue of Zeus at Olympia; the Hanging Gardens of Babylon; the Lighthouse at Alexandria and the Mausoleum at Halicarnassus). When Dame Freya Stark visited in 1952 she recorded: 'Sad hillocks of archaeological mud surround it, where fig trees grow on the bare ground and a man is ploughing of lives long past.'

Ephesians saw Artemis as a protector of their city. When Croe-

Rural living

sus, King of the Lydians, declared war on Ephesus, Ephesians tied the city to the Statue of Artemis in the holy shrine by rope, believing the line would provide divine protection and save the city from destruction. The Ephesians put up no fight, allowing Croesus's army to march right in to the city. Strangely, the Lydian king did not harm the vanquished city and its people. In fact, Ephesus became a more prosperous city during his brief reign.

The first Temple of Artemis was probably destroyed by the Cimmerians, a warrior race who attacked Ephesus in the 7th century BC. The oldest relics associated with the temple date to the 8th century BC and are now in the British Museum. The Great Temple of Artemis was built between 550BC and 460BC; it was the biggest structure ever built of marble. A total of 127 Ionic columns, each 19 metres (20 yards) high, supported a roof enclosing a courtyard 155 metres (172 yards) long by 55 metres (61 yards) wide. It was even more impressive than the rival Temple of Hera in Samos and four times larger than the Parthenon in Athens.

The temple was rebuilt after it was burned down in 356BC by an Ephesian seeking immortality. The second major Artemesion, built between 350 and 250BC, was almost identical to the first except that it was elevated on a base 3 metres (10ft) high with 13 steps.

The temple had to be reconstructed again after it was destroyed by Goths who attacked Ephesus in AD125 and again in AD262. With the growth of Christianity the cult of Artemis was replaced by adoration of the Virgin Mary. Marble from the Artemesion was used in the construction of Haghia Sophia (the grand Aya Sofya Basil-

Isa Bey Mosque

ica in Istanbul) and the Church of St John on the hill in Selçuk.

Drive up to the **Church of St John**, a key Christian shrine and a place of pilgrimage, constructed during the reign of Byzantine Emperor Justinian (AD527–65). For several centuries this church was visited by pilgrims and the sick, who hoped its dust would miraculously heal them.

It is believed that the grave located underneath the church belonged to St John, one of Christ's 12 disciples who lived the remaining years of his life in Ephesus after fleeing Jerusalem with the Virgin Mary. The church stands near the **Citadel of Selçuk**.

Even before the Church of St John was built there was a Baptistry in use here. The circular pool where baptisms were performed had a marble floor and was originally covered by a dome with a glass mosaic. Towards the eastern end of the church, at the end of the central nave just west of the apse, is the so-called **Tomb of St John**. The burial platform, two steps below the floor, used to be covered by a small dome. The marble mosaics adorning the platform have been restored.

The fortification wall surrounding the church was built in the 7th and 8th centuries to protect Ephesus against Arab invaders. At the main entrance to the church, the **Persuit Gate** and its adjoining courtyard were also built for defensive purposes. Invaders who penetrated this section could be shut in and killed by the defenders positioned along the walls.

Nearby is the **Isa Bey Mosque**. Erected in 1375 by Selçuk sultan Isa Bey, it occupies a vast area at the western base of the hill where the church of St John stands. This double-domed mosque has three chambers. Three original minarets still stand above the main entrance. Surrounding the large inner courtyard are unusually high walls which were partially constructed with marble from Ephesus.

Next drive to the **Grotto of the Seven Sleepers**, located in the valley below, 500 metres (547 yards) east of the Vedius Gymnasium. This is one of a number of sites associated with one of the early Christian myths. According to the story, around AD250 seven Christian boys fleeing persecution sought refuge in the cave. When they woke up 200 years later, Christianity had become the official religion and Emperor Theodosius proclaimed their resurrection. Afterwards, drive 8km (5 miles) from the Magnesian Gate into the hills to visit the **House of the Virgin Mary** (Meryemana in Turk-

House of the Virgin Mary

ish), where Mary purportedly lived from AD37–48. The serene setting, located in a forest set high in the hills, is believed by many Church scholars to be where St John brought the Virgin Mary after the Crucifixion. Officially recognised by the Vatican as the last residence of the Virgin Mother, the shrine has become a tourist attraction in recent years. Souvenir shops, outdoor coffeehouses and restaurants line the path to the house, which is now used as a chapel.

The search for the house began after a visionary dream by a German nun, Catherine Emmerich. In 1891, a search party led by the Lazarist friars discovered the House of the Blessed Virgin in a pine forest just before an *ayazma*, a sacred spring. Since its restoration in 1951, this modest stone house has been visited by two popes and millions of pilgrims, both Christian and Muslim (the Virgin Mary is also considered a Muslim saint). On 15 August a mass commemorating the Assumption of Mary is celebrated in the chapel.

After visiting the shrine, relax over a beverage at one of the coffeehouses under the trees and then drive back to Selçuk and on to the resort of **Kuşadası**, 18km (11 miles) away, for dinner.

A bright town with scores of carpet shops, leatherware stores and jewellers, Kuşadası has a large harbour and faces the Greek island of Samos, 2km (1 mile) away. The most interesting site is the Bird Island, a rocky structure on which a Genoese fortress stands. Connected to the mainland by a 400-metre (1,320-ft) causeway, the island has several pleasant outdoor coffeehouses. Built in AD1500,

the fortress later became home of Barboros Hayretttin Pasha, the Algerian pirate and grand admiral of the Ottoman navy under Süleyman the Magnificent.

The best restaurants are around the harbour and specialise in seafood. They include **Kazım Usta** (tel: 0256-6141226) or the **Ali Baba** (tel: 0256-6141551). After dinner drive back to

Kuşadası at dusk

Bodrum, or stay in Kuşadası for the night. The best hotels are the **Kısmet**, owned by Lady Hümeyra, an elderly Ottoman princess, and the **Kervansaray**, in the centre of town, in what was the **Öküz Mehmet Pasha Caravansaray**, an historic inn.

5. A Three-day Blue Voyage

A cruise in the Gulf of Gökova. On the first day, sail to Yedi Adalar (the Seven Islands); on the second, to the English Harbour; and on the third, to Cedar Islands.

—For the addresses of of agents where you can book a Blue Voyage, see Practical Information, page 88—

A Blue Voyage is the ultimate experience in relaxation for those harried by the stress of modern city life. One Turkish tourist official describes the Blue Voyage as a philosophical journey through time, when one can contemplate the early civilisations of mankind, explore the great beauty of the coast and marvel at its fasci-

Take to the ocean

nating marine life. 'Failure to journey into the Gulf of Gökova while visiting Bodrum,' wrote the Fisherman of Halicarnassus, 'would be like going up to the gate of a palace and not entering.'

Your boat has a captain, a cook and a dishwasher. All provisions are bought by the crew and stored on board. One of the most popular voyages begins with a two-hour trip to **Yedi Adalar** (Seven Islands), a secluded bay on the southeast corner of the Gulf of Gökova ringed by seven islands. To get there, the captain cuts across the 72-km (45-mile) long Gulf of Gökova after passing Karaada and Orak Adası (Sickle Island). To the right (south) are Datça Peninsula and the Greek island of Kos, and to the left (north) the cliffs east of Bodrum.

Upon reaching Yedi Adalar, the captain anchors the boat in the bay. While the cook prepares the meals, you can laze away the day, swimming, snorkelling, fishing or playing backgammon in the shade.

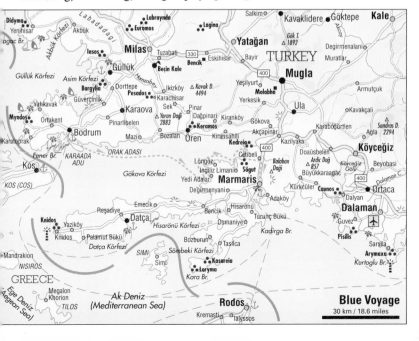

Messing about in boats

The next day at dawn, the boat sails for **Löngöz**, a deep, fiord-like bay about one-hour's distance from the Seven Islands, where it stops for breakfast and lunch, with swimming in between. The bay, engulfed by pine-clad hills and reed marshes, is a good place to search for marine life. After lunch, the boat continues to **Ingiliz Limanı**, the English Harbour, a long bay with safe mooring. The site gained its name in World War II when British naval patrol boats hid here during raids on the German-controlled Greek Aegean Islands. In 1988, Turkish scuba divers discovered the remains of two British Royal Air Force planes here, with the skeletons of the crew still inside. The war planes had been shot down by German anti-aircraft guns. If you skin-dive around the mouth of Ingiliz Limanı you may spot the wrecks of the aircraft. Afterwards swim across the bay to the restaurant-cum-coffeehouse for late afternoon tea.

The next morning the boat leaves for the **Sedir Islands**. Sedir means cedar and is named after the ancient city of **Cedrae** on the main island, scene of the great romance between Antony and Cleopatra. You will be rowed ashore at **Cleopatra's Beach** on the far side of the island Antony is said to have transported the fine silt sand of the beach from the Nile River to satisfy Cleopatra's whim.

After swimming, explore the ruins of Cedrae, which include parts of the city walls and an amphitheatre with gnarled olive trees breaking through the stone seatings and stage. The remains of a Doric temple, believed to be a sanctuary of Apollo, are also visible. Across the bay is a small island with a necropolis of tombs, known as the Snake Island. Little is known about Cedrae, an ancient Carian settlement. After the Spartans sacked the town during the Peloponnesian War in the 5th century BC it became completely Hellenised. It was finally abandoned in the Arab invasions in the 7th century.

From Cedrae, your boat heads for **Karacasöğüt**. The hamlet has several makeshift piers where boats can moor. Karacasöğüt is located on a big bay fringed by pine forests and holiday homes. It has two outdoor tavernas and several grocery stores. Its bay is ideal for windsurfing, swimming and rowing. Have dinner with other yachtsmen at the harbour taverna, which has authentic Turkish music and belly dancing until the morning hours. Leave around 11pm by taxi to Marmaris, a 25-mile (40-km) drive.

Marmaris

Marmaris has come a long way since it was levelled by a devastating earthquake in 1957. Once a tiny fishermen's outpost isolated from the rest of Turkey, the town was completely reconstructed following the quake. Today Marmaris is one of Turkey's most popular holiday resorts and the eastern Mediterranean's main yachting centre. Its marina has about 1,450 berths.

Located in an 8-km- (5-mile-) long, 3.2-km- (2-mile-) wide bay, picturesquely framed by pine forests and fragrant oleander shrubs that cascade down to the shore, the city lies at the confluence of the Aegean and the Mediterranean. Two islands protect the bay, making it an ideal place for windsurfing, water-skiing, jet skiing, sailing and other watersports.

The town is built around a 16th-century Ottoman citadel. Many of the town's banks, restaurants and souvenir shops are situated along the palm-lined Kordon Caddesi and Barbaros Caddesi at the northwestern end of the bay. The main shopping centre comprises several side streets that run off Cumhuriyet Meydanı (Republic Square) and the Atatürk Statue in front of the citadel and the Old Quarter. These shops sell everything, from carpets and leather goods to provisions for yachts.

Marmaris and bay

The town's name is said to be a corruption of the phrase '*Mimari as*' (hang the architect), the words reputedly uttered by Süleyman the Magnificent when he saw the puny fortifications of the town's castle as he prepared to use it as a springboard for his campaign to conquer Rhodes in 1522.

The citadel was originally constructed by Ionians who settled here in 3000BC. It was repaired by Alexander the Great in the 4th century BC and expanded by Süleyman the Magnificent in 1522AD. In 1798, the British grand admiral Horatio Nelson sheltered his entire fleet in the bay before vanquishing Napoleon's armada at the Battle of Aboukir.

A full day's boating excursion to Çiftlik, outside Marmaris Bay; visit Nimara Peninsula and Paradise Beach; swim in the Phosphorescent Grotto; stopover in Turunç Village and Kumlu Bükü Bay; return to Marmaris via İçmeler.

Spend your first day in Marmaris by taking a boat to **Çiftlik** (the Farm). It takes two hours to get to Çiftlik, which has the best and cleanest beach around Marmaris, and motor launches leave Marmaris quay, along Kordon Caddesi, at 9am. Those who can afford it are advised to charter a boat of their own: though more expensive, this avoids the noise of 30 others on a shared boat. The launches cruise along the northeastern part of the bay, hugging the shoreline.

To the left is the **Günnücek Park** with its fragrant conifers. After rounding **Bedir Island**, the boat comes to a stop at a little hidden cove aptly named **Cennet** (Paradise,) surrounded by a lush forest of pine trees. Cennet is part of the **Nimara Peninsula**, a bulging land mass that shelters the wide bay. The boat will stay for 20 minutes, allowing time to swim ashore to the sandy beach.

Continuing with the voyage, the boat rounds the Nimara Peninsula. Make sure the captain takes you behind the peninsula to the **Phosphorescent Grotto**, sometimes referred to as the Pirate's Cave. The boat can only enter the tiny cavern partially but it's sufficient to see the shiny bottom. Plunge in for a quick swim.

Leaving the grotto, the boat cuts across the sea to **Turunç Bükü**, a once lovely bay that has been ruined by construction, and sails to **Kumlu Bükü**, so far relatively unspoiled. Sometimes the boat will stop at both bays to drop or collect passengers. Next the boat glides by a long, rocky coastline that is completely uninhabited, finally stopping off at **Gerbekse**, a lovely cove with ruins of several Byzantine churches. If you feel the inclination, wade ashore and explore.

Çiftlik Bay

Float in crystal-clear waters

Afterwards the boat turns back and goes to Çiftlik, a bay protected by a craggy island on which an Istanbul businessman has built his very own castle. The waters of Çiftlik's 2-km (1-mile) long beach are crystal-clear. Except for a big hotel, several summer cottages and three farm-house restaurants, the bay is deserted. Enjoy *shish kebabı*, salad and melons at the pleasant farmhouse restaurant owned by Mehmet Yılmaz and his family, who are renowned for their hospitality. You have about two hours on Çiftlik before your boat begins its return journey.

Leaving Çiftlik, the boat passes Kumlu Bükü and Turunç Bükü and enters Marmaris Bay, stopping off at Içmeler, which has several big hotels, including the five-star Munamar and Aqua hotels and the nearby Martı Holiday Village. Continuing along the coast, the boat passes the luxurious Mares Hotel (formerly the Altın Yunus), the Turban Holiday Village and the renovated Hotel Lidya. Your boat finally returns to Marmaris around 6pm.

Spend the rest of the afternoon wandering through the narrow streets of the Old Quarter and visiting the Ottoman castle overlooking the town, and taking in some early evening shopping. Most of the shops around the harbour stay open until 9pm, some longer. The best place to buy carpets in Marmaris is at **Bazaar 54** (Yat Limanı, 1). The company specialises in the manufacture of fine, handmade silk carpets, and can deliver anywhere in the world. Another carpet shop you may want to visit is **Silk Road**, in the marina. Attractive leather goods and sheepskin coats can be purchased at **Antilop Leather** (Halıcı Ishani,1).

For dinner, select one of the many outdoor seafood restaurants along the harbourfront. Afterwards, head for one of the bars and pubs, the best of which is **Keyif Bar** (Netsel Marina), from where you have a good view of Marmaris and the marina. If you are up to it, you may want to end your

Local colour

evening at a disco. One of the most popular is the disco of the Martı Hotel at Içmeler. The **Ezgi Cafe Bar** (Yat Limanı) provides Anatolian music, with its owner Ali Örüç playing Turkish instruments and singing folk tunes.

A drive to the ancient city of Knidos; stop at Datça; visit ruins of Knidos and the temple of Aphrodite; lunch at Baba Restaurant; visit Palamut's quiet bay for swimming; return to Marmaris for dinner.

On your second day in Marmaris drive to the ruins of **Knidos**, an ancient Carian city at the tip of the Datça Peninsula, west of Marmaris. Rent a car, preferably a four-wheel drive, as some of the roads are in a bad condition. It takes three hours to drive the 95km (59 miles) from Marmaris to Knidos. You should leave by 8am and try to get back to Marmaris before dark to avoid the treacherous meandering road at night. If you cannot make it before nightfall, spend the night at Datça. Make sure your vehicle has spare tyres before you leave.

The drive to Knidos is scenic. After Içmeler, the asphalt road winds into the mountains for about 20km (12 miles) only to drop gently to the fertile plains and the **Hisarönü Bay** below. The Datça Peninsula, a spiny, 72-km (45-mile) long, finger-like projection separates the Hisarönü Bay in the south from the Gökova Bay in the north. Soon you reach the Datça Peninsula and its narrowest point, which is named **Balıkaşıran** (the place where fish leap across); here the isthmus is less than a mile wide. For the next 32km (20 miles), the road is a series of hairpin turns from which both bays can be viewed from dizzying heights.

Datça marina

Halfway up the peninsula is Datça, a popular stopover for yachtsmen. The town has many seafood restaurants, pensions and hotels, of which the Hotel Olimpos (tel: 0252-7122001), on the tiny peninsula, is one of the best. Across the bay, the Greek island of Symi, or Sömbeki in Turkish, is visible, only 11km (7 miles) away. Daily ferry boats make excursions to Datça from Bodrum. Have a tea break at Datça before moving on. Daily boat trips from Datça to Knidos are less tiring than driving, with stops in many secluded bays. However, the return journey is at sundown, requiring travellers to spend the night in Datça.

A few miles out of Datça, the road is unpaved as it climbs the rugged vertebrae of a new mountain chain, passing villages, almond orchards and olive groves. It takes about one hour to reach windswept Knidos from Datça.

Once a thriving commercial port, **Knidos** is now in ruins. Except for a lone *bekçi* or night watchman who guards the ancient site, and three ramshackle fish restaurants, the old city is deserted.

Temple of Aphrodite

The ruins of this once mighty 4th-century BC city face the open sea and the Hisarönü and Gökova bays. A series of Greek islands, including Cos, Yiali, Nisiros, Khalki and Rhodes, which hug the Turkish mainland, are visible from Knidos.

The ancient city once housed a beautiful statue of Aphrodite, considered at the time to be the finest work of art in the world. The statue has long since disappeared, perhaps destroyed in an earthquake or yet to be discovered by archaeologists. The round foundation of the temple where it stood, on top of the hill commanding a grand view of both bays, can be reached after a short walk. The ruins also include the remains of an acropolis, two harbours, terraced houses, a necropolis of Roman tombs and two amphitheatres.

For lunch, walk back to the harbour and have fish or *istakoz,* a tasty lobster, at **Baba Restaurant**.

After lunch, drive to the village of **Palamut**, 13km (8 miles) away, facing the Hisarönü Bay, to swim in its long, deserted beach. Palamut, which means 'bonito' in Turkish, gets its name from the abundance of fish caught in the bay. The village is the site of the ancient Knidian city of Triopium. It was in this ancient city that Dorian states held sporting events in honour of Apollo, the Greek God of manly youth and beauty, that were precursors to the Olympic Games. An acropolis and some ruins lie above the village, but only those with a serious interest in ruins are likely to find them worth the climb.

Return to Marmaris along the same roads. In the evening, enjoy the city's sunset and colourful nightlife over a leisurely meal at one of the many restaurants in the harbour.

Local inhabitant

Boating at Dalyan

8. Boating Trip to Caunos and Dalyan

A boating excursion to Caunos and Dalyan; stop off at Ekincik; change boats to go up the Dalyan River; visit the Caunos ruins. Spend the night at Dalyan to see the giant loggerhead turtles and the following day hire a car from Dalyan airport to take you to Fethiye, springboard for the next itineraries in this book.

Daily motorboats to **Caunos** and **Dalyan** leave at 8.30am from the quay along Kordon Caddesi. The journey takes four hours.

After leaving Marmaris Bay, the boat turns left, rounds Nimara Peninsula and follows the rocky coastline eastward. You are now in the Mediterranean. At times the sea gets choppy, but the trip is usually pleasant. You can get beer and soft drinks aboard the boat, but you must pay for these separately.

About two hours out of Marmaris, on your left you pass the mouth of **Aksaz Limanı**, a wide bay which is a military zone. Stopping at the mouth of the bay, entering it, or taking pictures in the zone are absolutely forbidden.

One hour after leaving Aksaz Limanı, you reach the pretty **Ekincik Bay** and **Delikada** island. The island stands at the mouth of the narrow, twisting **Dalyan River** and the remote **Iztuzu Beach**, popularly known as Turtle Beach. Resembling a vast sandbar, the 5-km (3-mile) long beach is one of the Mediterranean's few remaining

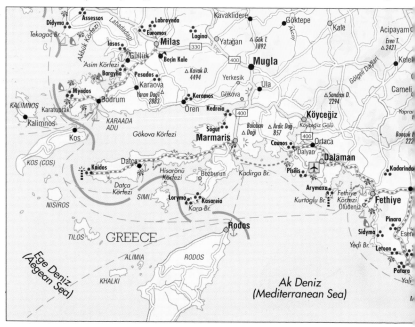

breeding grounds for the Loggerhead Marine Turtle (*Caretta Caretta*).

At Ekincik Bay, passengers must transfer to smaller boats that can navigate the shallow Dalyan River to Caunos. The boat ride takes about half an hour through marshlands and a delta surrounded by tall reeds. On the way to Caunos, you will notice many fisheries which trap *kefal* (mullet) and *levrek* (sea bass). These breeds can live in both salt and freshwater; they are caught returning to the sea after spawning at **Köyceğiz Gölü**, which is upstream. The name Dalyan, just across the river from Caunos, means 'fishery'.

Get off at the small boat landing and walk up to the ancient Carian city of Caunos, whose ruins are scattered on two levels. Caunos was once a thriving port, but is now in ruins. Its downfall came with the silting up of its harbour by the Dalyan river and an outbreak of malaria. Among the ruins are an amphitheatre, an acropolis hill, and a series of Lycian Tombs, hewn into the cliff on the other side of the site, facing the Dalyan river. From the top of the hill, you can see the village of Dalyan.

Return to another boat landing, following a different trail that leads from the acropolis down the hill. At the bottom of the hill, your boat will collect you and take you across to a fish restaurant in Dalyan for lunch. You will not be returning with the others to Marmaris but staying in Dalyan for the night. There are several attractive restaurants along the river, but one of the best is the **Deniz Yıldızı** (the Star Fish), just off the main square.

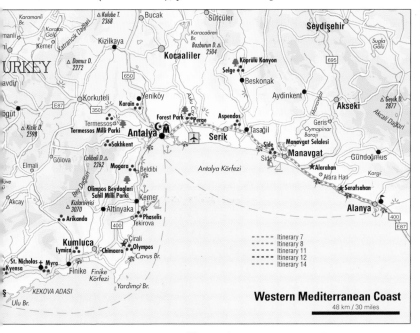

Western Mediterranean Coast

48 km / 30 miles

Choose your fish

For lunch try *kefal*, caught in the many fisheries along the river, together with various *meze* dishes, including fried eggplant steeped in tomato sauce. *Kefal*, a tasty grey mullet, is best served grilled. After lunch, take a taxi and check into one of the many pensions for the night. Dalyan is a quiet resort with no big hotels. Although there are many clean, modestly priced pensions in the village, the best are along the river. One that you may want to try is the Caretta Caretta Hotel, built by Nail Çakırhan, a poet and journalist who won an architectural award for a residence he constructed in true Turkish style.

After settling into your hotel, return to the village square and hire a boat to take you downstream to the **Turtle Beach**. The water is shallow and safe, and the beach is ideal for tossing frisbees, playing volleyball and building sandcastles.

During the June–September turtle breeding season, the beach is closed to the public from 6pm–9am to prevent tourists upsetting the turtles' nests. If you are visiting Dalyan during this period and want to see the turtles come ashore to lay their egg, you must get permission from the local authorities in town. A group of marine biologists, studying the turtles and usually camped about 2km (1 mile) from the mouth of the river behind the beach, along a marshy lake, may be able to help you get the necessary permit. In the afternoons, you will usually find them resting at the small outdoor coffeehouse on the beach by the river. Once you have the permit, return to Dalyan for the evening.

The village is one of the most relaxing locations in Turkey and evenings in Dalyan are lazy and calm. Have some *çay* (Turkish tea), soft drinks or beer at one of the outdoor cafés in front of the quay then go to one of the other fish restaurants by the river for dinner. Especially recommended is the *levrek* (sea bass), which can be served fried or grilled; also try some *pavurya* or *yengeç* (crabs) as an appetiser. The waiter will bring a small hammer to crack the shells.

Afterwards return to your hotel to get some sleep, for you will need to be up at 3am to take a taxi to Turtle Beach. Arrange a taxi before heading to your hotel (no car rental services are available in Dalyan). Dig out a sweater to take with you as the beach can be chilly before sunrise. The 15-km (9-mile) drive to Turtle Beach takes about 20 minutes.

Turkey's tiny environmentalist movement won its first major victory at Turtle Beach in 1987 when it pressurised the Turkish government to stop the building of a big Turkish-German hotel near the beach, on the grounds that the construction work would endanger the newly-hatched turtles. Today the beach is an environmentally protected area, and a night watchman keeps vigil to prevent locals and tourists from entering the area during the turtles' breeding season. Tell the watchman you are going to the camp of the marine biol-

Turtle Beach

ogists, who will show you around. You are not allowed to light matches or use flashlights, and must walk in the moonlight for about 2 miles (3km) to the camp. On your way, remember to look out for nests and be sure not trample on any: they are marked off with stakes.

If you are visiting during the breeding season, you will see some loggerhead turtles, even during the day. Scores, sometimes hundreds, of huge female loggerhead turtles, travelling from as far as West Africa, wade ashore at Iztuzu Beach in June and July and bury their eggs in the sand. It takes six to eight weeks for the baby turtles to hatch. Breaking out of their shells, they cling to one another like a double helix, claw their way up through the sand for air and then push on to the sea, a journey fraught with danger. Only one in every 10 reaches the sea. Hundreds of turtles are eaten by ghost crabs that lay traps in the sand. Hawks and other predatory birds catch any turtles that fail to reach the sea by daylight.

You can walk from one end of the beach to the other accompanied by the biologists in the early dawn as the sun breaks out of the eastern mountains. They will point out the nests and the footprints of the little turtles.

The next day take a cab to Dalaman International Airport, a 12-mile (20-km) drive through fertile farmlands of orange and tangerine orchards. Halfway to Dalaman is the town of **Ortaca**, famous for its cotton. At the airport (**Dalaman Hava Limanı**), rent a car for the rest of your trip. A number of international car rental services have bureaux at the airport, including **Avis**, tel: (0252) 6925410, and **Airtour**, tel: (0252) 6925979 or 6925291. Compare prices, and try to haggle.

From Dalaman, drive to the next big resort on the Turkish Coast, Fethiye, 56 miles (90km) away (return to the Muğla– Fethiye Highway, and turn right). The east-bound road soon climbs up pine-covered mountains, the beginning of ancient Lycia, only to come down suddenly to Göcek, at the northwestern end of the wide Fethiye Bay. Göcek has become an important yachting centre, with several five-star hotels. Continue to Fethiye, only one hour away.

Young farm hands

Fethiye

Immensely popular among French, German, Austrian and British tourists and yachtsmen of all nationalities, Fethiye is a centre for voyages into the Gulf of Fethiye, the Twelve Islands, and the region around Kekova Island, which has some of the most mysterious sunken cities in the world. The town is also the gateway to Lycia, famed for its rock tombs which date back more than 2,500 years.

Though Fethiye has always been an important centre for the export of chromium (Turkey is the world's biggest producer of this metal, which is mined all along the bulge of the Lycian coast), until 1950 it was no more than a minor market village with no road connections with any provincial capitals. At the time, all goods were transported by boat. The first organised tour group to visit Fethiye came on a boat trip from Rhodes in 1963.

The town dates back to the 6th century BC. It was once a Lycian city called Telmessus, and

The front at Fethiye

traces of the ancient settlement can be seen about the town, including the rock tombs on the face of a cliff east of the city and several scattered heavy sarcophagi, such as the one next to the Town Hall. The town, however, is modern, reconstructed after the earthquakes of 1950 and 1957, which levelled it completely. Even so it makes a very agreeable base; in spite of tourism development, it remains low-key.

Situated at the eastern end of the big Gulf of Fethiye, the town is surrounded by mountains that are snowcapped in winter. A bulging headland and an island known as Şövalyeler Adası (the Knights' Island) embrace the town, providing ideal shelter for yachts.

An afternoon visit to the Rock Tomb of Amyntas, a stroll through Kaya Ghost Town, and return to Fethiye; see the sarcophagus.

After settling into your hotel, drive to the rock tombs just behind the city. Park your car at the base of the cliffs and walk up a steep path to these fine monuments of the dead, the most magnificent of which is the **Temple Tomb of Amyntas**, a Lycian notable. The Lycians, a seafaring people known for their exceptional bravery and the staunch defence of their freedom, revered their dead, carving many such tombs into mountains all over southwest Turkey. An acropolis hill at the back of the town is occupied by a castle, believed to have been constructed by the Knights of St John.

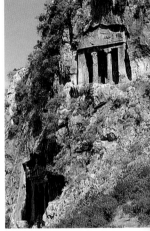

Return to your car and drive up the mountain past the rock tombs to **Kaya Ghost Town**. You will soon pass a sarcophagus in the middle of the road. None of the rock tombs or sarcophagi were damaged or even budged during the earthquakes that flattened Fethiye in 1950 and 1957. The local denizens have never considered moving the sarcophagus in the middle of the road, claiming that if it were to move even slightly, 'the whole world would shake'.

The dirt road curves into the mountains for about 10km (6 miles), passing dense pine and

Tomb of Amyntas

cedar forests, and winds down to a fertile plain. Kaya, formerly known as Kormylassos, stands on a hill overlooking the plain.

ÇALIŞ BEACH

Fethiye Körfezi

100 Yıl Caddesi

Club Mediterranee

Stadyumu (Stadium)

Government Building

Belediye Binasi (Municipal Building)
Police
Post Office
Atatürk Caddesi

Quay

Customs and Passport Police

Tourist Information

Hamam (Turkish Bath)

Shopping Centre
Theatre Cavea

Çarşı Caddesi

Lycian Ruins and Tombs

Lycian Ruins and Tombs

Lycian Ruins and Tombs

Fortress

Lycian Ruins and Tombs

Lycian Rock Tombs

I. KARAGÖZLER

Lycian Ruins and Tombs

Fevzi Çakmak Caddesi

II. KARAGÖZLER

Fethiye

800m / 874 yds

Kaya Ghost Town

Kaya was once a wealthy Greek town of 5,000 people, the most populous in the region. The Greeks abandoned Kaya, as part of the general population exchanges between Greece and Turkey at the end of the Greco-Turkish War of 1919–22. Kaya is now an eerie ghost town. Hundreds of houses, with their roofs crumbled from the quakes, remain standing along rock paths. Two well-preserved churches, one built in 1888 and displaying frescoes of biblical scenes, remain intact.

Return to Fethiye along the same road. Stroll around the port and the Belediye Binası (Municipal building), next to which you will see a huge sarcophagus, and cross the street to browse in the shops. For dinner, head for **Rafet Restaurant**, indisputably the best seafood restaurant in town, along Kordonboyu (the quay), just off Atatürk Caddesi running north-south through the town. It specialises in grilled fish and offers a great choice of appetisers. Prices are modest and governed by the daily price of fish, written on a blackboard by the display refrigerator. Try some *orfoz* (dusky grouper) or *akya* (leer fish).

Afterwards, walk across the main street and take a look at the many shops along Çarsı Caddesi, which is parallel to Atatürk Caddesi. If you want to experience the town's nightlife drive to Club Letoonia Holiday Village, a sprawling holiday town across the bay on Paçaraz Peninsula, which serves both a Turkish and international clientele. It is only a 10-km (6-mile) drive. Park your car at the entrance and walk about 1km (½ mile) to the main bar along the middle promenade, passing the luxury homes of Turkey's nouveau riche and fancy apartment bungalows for guests.

From here, the flickering lights of Fethiye can be seen across the bay. The floodlit open-air bar is at the far end of the peninsula. After spending about an hour exploring the town, return to Fethiye for a nightcap at the cosy **Yasmin Bar** (Iskele Karsısı, tel: 0252-6121183), which occupies an old 19th-century Turco-Greek mansion. It serves good cocktails and has live music.

An excursion by boat into the Gulf of Fethiye to the Twelve Islands, stopping for swimming, picnics and snorkelling. Have tea at Göcek, and return to Fethiye for dinner at a Chinese restaurant.

The Gulf of Fethiye, with the Twelve Islands off Göcek, is one of the most secluded and beautiful areas on the Turkish Coast. Motorboat launches leave Fethiye quay (Kordonboyu) at 9am sharp. You can also charter a motorboat plus captain if you want complete privacy.

First stop is **Şövalyeler Adası** (the Knights' Island), sometimes also known as Fethiye Adası, across from Fethiye. To your right is the 4-km (2½-mile) long **Çaliş Beach**, one of the best beaches near Fethiye. To your left is a peninsula known as **Oyuk Tepe**. Club Mediterranée dominates one of its headlands.

The Knights' Island gets its romantic name from the Knights of St John who

Secluded mooring

are thought to have controlled it in the Middle Ages. The thin island has several beaches suitable for swimming and some pleasant privately-owned summer houses. The boat anchors offshore for about 20 minutes, allowing time for a quick swim.

The boat then leaves for the Twelve Islands on the western end of the Gulf of Fethiye. It takes about 90 minutes to reach the islands,

bypassing several uninhabited islands in the middle of the gulf. The first group of islands include **Yassıca Adaları**, which is good for mooring and swimming, and the larger **Hacıhalil Adası**. The boat doesn't usually stop at any of these islands, but continues to the big island on the left, **Tersane Adası**, which has a protected cove suitable for anchorage. The boat will stop for about half an hour, allowing time to swim ashore and explore. The ruins of several buildings face the cove. Tersane means 'shipyards' in Turkish – the Greek families who once lived on the island built wooden-framed boats.

From Tersane, the boat crosses the narrow strait to **Domuz Adası** (Pig's Island), owned by Erol Simavi, the publisher of Turkey's best-selling newspaper *Hürriyet* and one of the most powerful men in the country. Simavi's villa stands amidst what appears to be ancient ruins (stopping at the island is forbidden). Simavi has hosted many well-known guests at his secret island retreat, including members of the British Royal Family.

The boat continues to **Hamam Cove**, whose partially submerged ruins claim to be the **Baths of Cleopatra**. The boat will stop for 90 minutes in the bay. Have lunch at one of the alfresco restaurants (open only in summer), or explore the submerged ruins.

From Hamam Cove, the captain will take you to the westernmost point of the Gulf, **Bedri Rahmi Bay**, which derives its name from the cubist fish painting on a rock by the late Bedri Rahmi Eyüboğlu. The region is also known as **Taşyaka**, or **Tombs Bay**, on account of the many Lycian cemeteries and pigeon-hole rock tombs along the jagged shoreline. Your boat will stop here for about 30 minutes.

The next bay on your voyage to Göcek is **Boynuzbükü**, a deep sheltered bay surrounded by pine trees where sail boats can anchor safely. A river, lined with reeds and oleander shrubs, empties into the bay. The Turkish government recently banned the construction of several new hotels in this bay. As you head toward Göcek, you will pass two islands on your right, **Zeytinli Adası**, a privately owned estate with thousands of olive trees, and **Göcek Adası**, with its verdant pine forests.

As you enter the far end of the bay facing Göcek, look out for an old Istanbul steamboat ferry, *Halas*, docked by the shore and now used as a luxury hotel-restaurant. Ask the skipper to moor his boat alongside the other yachts at Göcek harbour for a short stay so that you can have afternoon tea at one of the seaside coffeehouses. In spite of having a population of just 2,000, Göcek is one of the few places in Turkey where you can buy newspapers and magazines from all over the world. The boat ride back to Fethiye takes about 90 minutes; you should be back by about 6.30pm.

For dinner in Fethiye, try the **Chinese Restaurant** near the marina. The food is excellent. If you plump for the duck, you may want to decline invitations to sit at the tables next to the harbour – the ducks are kept on a raft just below. Afterwards dip into the numerous bars around **Iskele Meydanı**, the main square, including **Otantik Bar** (Hamam Sok, Paspatur Mevkii), which offers live music in a restored Ottoman mansion, popular with local youth and tourists.

Home entertainment

Drive to Ölüdeniz (the Dead Sea) for swimming and parasailing, or paragliding from the top of the 1,976-metre (6,480-ft) Baba Dağ. In the afternoon, a drive to Letoon; Xanthos city and Patara ruins. Spend the night in Kaş.

Leave your hotel around 8.30am and drive to **Ölüdeniz**, the 'Dead Sea', 15km (9 miles) from Fethiye. The turn-off to Ölüdeniz is on the right as you drive to the Muğla–Antalya Highway.

Ölüdeniz appear to be a perfectly calm lagoon, though it actually has a small mouth opening to the sea from which boats can enter. Though an ideal shelter for yachts, ringed by mountains, pine trees and a long sandy beach, Ölüdeniz has been closed to yachts since 1984 to prevent pollution of its crystal-clear waters. The **Belcekız Beach** along the lagoon is one of the best sand beaches

of Turkey (it becomes deep very fast, however, and is not suitable for small children). Because of this it is crowded and noisy in the summer: scores of camp sites and motels have opened in the past decade along the beach, and more are being built in the mountains.

Ölüdeniz

As well as swimming at Belcekız Beach, you can parasail – there are several parasailing clubs. You can also try paragliding from the top of Baba Dağ, a rocky peak of 1,976metres (6,480ft) dominating the coast. Deniz Camping, a camping site with bungalows, arranges flights from Baba Dağı to Belcekız Beach, a 25-minute parachute glide.

After swimming and sunbathing, have lunch at Deniz Camping, owned and operated by Hülya Gürkan (a British woman whose real name is Anthea), her son Osman, and her husband, a former Turkish Air Force pilot. The Gürkans have been operating the camp site for over 20 years and were the first to open such facilities on the beach. They have also restored 25 houses in the abandoned former Greek village of **Ocakköy** in the mountains and turned them into a motel village complex. The pleasant village, with its library, outdoor pool, bar and do-it-yourself craft shop, is located halfway between Ölüdeniz and Fethiye. It is also the place to take a donkey ride along mountain trails.

After lunch, drive back to the Fethiye–Antalya Highway, turning toward Antalya. You will drive for about one hour to your next destination, **Letoon**, the ancient sanctuary of the goddess Leto,

Boys in Letoon

mother of both Artemis and Apollo and the mistress of Zeus. Past the town of Esen and the village of Hazırlar take the road on the right to Letoon. The shrine is about 5km (3 miles) off the main road. Leto was the principal goddess of the Lycians, who inhabited this rugged part of Anatolia more than 2,000 years ago. The ruins contain the foundations of three temples, the main one dedicated to Leto, and the others to Artemis and Apollo. They also contain a nymphaion (a kind of public bath) partially submerged in water, and a well-preserved amphitheatre. In the middle of the Temple of Apollo, you can see a mosaic of a lyre, the sun, and a bow and arrow, the only known mosaic of the Lycian civilisation.

Return to the main road and drive to **Xanthos** 5km (3 miles) away. Xanthus, the most impressive and important Lycian city, is just off the Fethiye–Antalya highway, near the village of Kınık, along the Xanthos River (known today as Esen Çayı). A dirt road leads into the ruins. On the left as you enter the site you will see an outstanding amphitheatre, and next to it two tombs. The so-called **Harpies Tomb**, an elevated funerary monument, gets its name from reliefs showing the mythological harpies, half-birds, half-women monsters, carrying dead children to the underworld. Next to it is the **Pillar Tomb**, a squat Lycian sarcophagus on top of a long, rectangular pillar. Facing the amphitheatre is the agora on which stands the famous **Xanthian Steele,** a pillar tomb whose frame is covered with 250 lines of Lycian script, the longest ever discovered, and a Greek poem. On the other side of the road are ruins of two Byzantine basilicas and a monastery.

The early history of Xanthos is obscure. It made its mark during the Persian General Harpagus's invasion of the southwestern coast of Asia Minor around 540BC. Defeated by Harpagus in battle, the Lycians, rather than surrender Xanthus, gathered their wives and children in the acropolis, which they set ablaze in a defiant act of mass suicide.

The Xanthians re-enacted the tragedy 500 years later during the Roman Civil Wars. In 42BC, when Brutus, attempting to raise money for his showdown with Antony and Octavian, arrived

Detail in Xanthos

in Xanthos, he faced opposition from the Lycians who withdrew into the city and attempted to defend the walls. But when the forces of Brutus broke through the walls and the city capitulated, the Xanthians slaughtered their families, built a big pyre in the centre of the city and threw themselves into the flames.

In both cases, some Xanthians must have survived for the city was again populated during the Byzantine period. Its end most likely came during the Arab invasions of Anatolia in the 7th century.

Xanthos was discovered by Sir Charles Fellows in 1838. Four years later, sailors from the British Navy, under Lieutenant Thomas Spratt's command, removed hundreds of statues and friezes from the site in what Turks today describe as a rape of the nation's archaeological wealth. All the statuary removed from Xanthus are now in the British Museum.

Return to the Fethiye–Antalya Highway, continuing towards Antalya. Drive along to **Patara**, which also has one of the best beaches in Turkey. The ruins are located 10km (6 miles) from Xanthos (turn right at the yellow sign pointing toward the ancient site). Patara is the traditional birthplace of St Nicholas, the gift-bearing Santa Claus associated with the snowy winters of northern Europe. It was once a great commercial port, but today is partially covered by sand dunes and hidden by an almost impenetrable forest of thick bushes and trees, about 0.5km (¼ mile) from the sea. The town is now being systematically excavated.

As you enter Patara, you will pass an arch. Park your car in front of the restaurant, behind the beach. The nearby amphitheatre is half-filled with sand. On the knoll between the beach and the theatre stands an unusual structure believed to be some kind of water cistern. Next to it are ruins of what may have been a lighthouse. Next to the harbour is the well-preserved **Granary of Hadrian**. Patara was famous for its Oracle of Apollo, vying with the Oracle of Delphi as the centre of prophecy in the ancient world, but no trace of this building has ever come to light.

If it is not too late in the day, take a dip in Patara's 18-km (11-mile) long sandy beach. But beware: as it faces the open sea, Patara's waters can be turbulent and a strong undertow makes Patara's sea dangerous, especially for youngsters. After a quick swim, drive to the resort of Kaş, about 60km (37 miles) from Patara on the Fethiye–Antalya highway, passing **Kalkan**, an attractive village becoming popular among sun-seeking holidaymakers. The road to Kaş winds along the coast, passing many small sandy beaches on the way.

Like most towns on the Lycian coast, **Kaş** is wedged between mountains and the sea. In recent years, it has become a popular stopover for yachts on the Blue Voyage. It faces the tiny island of Kastellorizon (Meis in Turkish), the farthest Greek island from mainland Greece. Meis, a resort island, gets all its supplies from Kaş and its hotel owners speak fluent Turkish. Each morning, motorboats from Meis come to Kaş for supplies.

Kaş is also the centre for boat trips to the sunken cities around **Kekova Island** and the fishing village

Sleepy day in Kaş

Barbecue time in Kaş

of **Kale**, famous for its necropolis of Lycian tombs. This is a full-day trip – boats leave for Kale from Kaş each morning at 9am.

As you will be spending the night in Kaş, book into a hotel. There are several possibilities in the town, but the **Ekici Hotel**, tel: (0242) 8361417, overlooking the port, and the **Aqua-Park Hotel**, tel: (0242) 8361901, at Çukurbağ Peninsula, are most comfortable.

Kaş was the location for the ancient city **Antiphellos**, but scant remains of the old settlement have survived. There are several sarcophagi about the town, including one by the port and an elevated one on the square above **Uzunçarşı Caddesi** which features the heads of lions on its sides. An ancient amphitheatre is situated on Kaş's long peninsula, just a short walk from the town.

Spend the early evening shopping in the bazaar area, where there are numerous gift shops and then have dinner at one of the many fish restaurants by the port, lined with visiting yachts. The restaurants of the region are well-known for serving goat's meat, a local delicacy, instead of mutton or beef. One caveat: make certain prices are clearly listed; several restaurants in Kaş have a reputation for overcharging gullible tourists.

12. A Drive to Antalya

Visit St Nicholas Church in Demre and explore the Myra ruins; drive to the pirates' hideout of Olympus to picnic among the ruins and swim at the beach. Visit the eternal flames at Yanartaş; pass Kemer, and explore the Old City in Antalya.

Leave Kaş in the early morning and drive into the mountains to Antalya, your final destination. About 50km (30 miles) from Kaş is the farming community of **Demre**, famous for its juicy tomatoes. It was at Demre, known to the ancients as **Myra**, that St Nicholas, the original Santa Claus, a legendary man of good deeds lived and worked in the 4th century. The Church recognises St Nicholas as a genuine historical figure, the first Bishop of Myra. The ruins of ancient Myra, complete with an amphitheatre and rock cemeteries, are about 1km (½ mile) out of town and are visible from every point.

Since Myra was a port as well as a farming town, St Nicholas was originally the patron saint of sailors. **St Nicholas Church**, where he purportedly delivered sermons, is a Muslim as well as a Christian shrine – among Turks St Nicholas

Statue of St Nicholas

is known as 'Noel Baba' (Father Christmas). To get to the church, follow the yellow sign that says 'Noel Baba'; a statue of the saint, surrounded by children, stands in the courtyard. Though the saint's marble sarcophagus lies inside the church, in the 11th century pirates removed the remains to Bari, a town on Italy's Adriatic Coast.

In early December Church scholars and amateur historians from around the world gather in Kaş to attend the world's only Santa Claus Symposium. During the three-day seminar, scholars discuss the character and life of the saint and trace his development as a Christian figure. On 6 December, priests from the Orthodox Church Patriarchate in Istanbul hold two-hour liturgical services at the small church in honour of St Nicholas. The services and symposium coincide with Demre's St Nicholas Festival, held 1–7 December. If you want further details about the symposium, you can contact the Tourism Office in Kaş, tel: (0242) 8361238.

From the church drive to the ruins of Myra, following the sign. Park by the gates and walk in. Myra's big amphitheatre, the first structure you come to, is of Roman style. In the west gallery is the inscription 'Place of vendor Gelasius', and this was probably the stand where theatre-goers could buy nuts and other edibles to nibble on while watching a performance. Myra has the most impressive rock tombs on the entire Lycian Coast. The cliff facing Myra is honeycombed with rock graves, giving it a gloomy sepulchral atmosphere (to reach the tombs, follow the trail up to the cliffs). Many of these tombs have friezes of human figures

Myra's rock tombs

or graffiti. The most striking grave is known as the **Painted Tomb**, adorned with friezes of the man and his family presumed to be buried here.

Leave Demre and drive to **Finike**, about 40km (25 miles) to the east. Finike, which is Turkey's leading orange-producing community, is a market town by a river. In recent times, it has become a popular stopover for yachtsmen who need to pick up provisions. Just before the town is a wide cove known as **Andrea Doria Bay**, named after the 16th-century Venetian admiral who is said to have concealed his flagship in the bay while fighting the Ottoman navy. There isn't much to see in the town, and its long sandy beach is unpleasant, cluttered with tons of soggy, rotting oranges thrown from nearby orange packaging plants.

The weather gets so sultry and humid in summer here that townspeople and villagers move to the cool mountain plateaux, where

The beach at Olympos

many have summer cottages. The best hotel in town is the **Baykal Motel Pension** (tel: 0242-8551774), the only motel in Turkey where the owner personally provides a free taxi service for guests from town to the pension.

Before leaving town, buy some groceries, including drinking water and beverages, for a picnic lunch at the next stop, the ancient city of **Olympos**.

For the next 20km (12 miles), drive along the coast, past the town of **Kumluca**. The road winds up into mountains blanketed by tall pine and cedar trees. Take the old Finike–Antalya highway and turn right at a sign to Çavuş and Olympos, and drive for about 2km (1 mile). Turn left at the Olympos sign. A poorly paved road, 7km (4 miles) long, full of potholes, takes you to the ancient town. Drive carefully if you don't have a four-wheel drive: there are no service stations near here.

Olympos, a city now in ruins, is located in a gorge between two steep mountains. A stream runs through the town, once a pirate's hideout, and the ruins spread over both banks, covered by a jungle of bushes and trees. Olympos, which probably means mountain in a pre-Greek language, is one of some 20 sites and mountains in the eastern Mediterranean with that name. The town has never been excavated. Nearly 2,000 years ago, pirates controlled the settlement, raiding and plundering the commercial ships plying the coast.

You can see parts of the city's quay (on the southern bank of the stream) and the remains of a theatre by fording across the knee-deep water. The main section of the city spreads

Olympos tomb

along the northern bank, and you can still see an acropolis on the hill by the beach. Several tiny sarcophagi, probably for children, stand with their lids partly open on the side of the hill. You can also still see the walls of what were probably residential houses on the northern bank along the river. The main necropolis is on the southern side of the river bank and has many ornate tombs.

Unpack your lunch in the shade of the trees along the river bank and afterwards have a dip in the sea, just 200 metres/yards from the entrance of the settlement.

Afterwards return to your car and drive to the village of **Çiralı** to visit the eternal flames of **Yanartaş** (the Burning Stone), on the face of a mountain. To get to Çiralı, return to the Finike–Antalya highway and turn toward Antalya. You will soon reach the new highway. Turn right at the Çiralı sign; the dirt road goes downhill for about 5km (3 miles). Turn left at the small coffeehouse and drive for another mile, then take the dirt road on the left that goes into the canyon and leave your car at the end of the road. You must walk the rest of the way, following a trail into the mountain. The climb to Yanartaş takes about 45 minutes. Be careful not to step on scorpions. The Yanartaş is an outcrop of rocks surrounded by pine trees.

The fires have been burning for thousands, perhaps millions, of years. The flames, according to myth, are the remains of the **Chimaera**, the fire-snorting monster that once terrorised the coastal area. The Chimera, which had a lion's head, a goat's body and a serpent's tail, was slain by mythical Lycian hero Bellerophon, who flew over the mountains with his winged horse Pegasus. Turkish scientists explain the fires by citing a build-up of underground methane gas that can't be extinguished. If you douse the flames with water, they will spring back in seconds. The whole area is volcanic and may harbour considerable oil reserves. The fires of the Chimera can be distinguished at night by vessels sailing along the coast.

Just below the Yanartaş are some unusual ruins believed to be a sanctuary for the fire god Hephaestus. One of the ruins strangely resembles a Byzantine chapel. Return to the highway and drive toward Antalya.

The road runs through **Olympus National Park** for over 70km (45 miles), passing through thick forests. To the left of the road is the **Bey Dağları**, a mountain range with impressively jagged peaks resembling the Rocky Mountains. Soon you pass the turnoff to the resort of **Kemer.** Benefiting from spectacular surroundings and the recipient of hefty World Bank loans, Kemer has evolved into a booming tourism centre.

Ancient **Phaselis** hugs the shore about 12 miles (20km) north of Olympos National Park, in the midst of a thick pine forest. Its beautiful setting combined with impressive avenues, amphitheatres, aqueducts and ancient tombs make it one of the most impressive archaeological sites in Turkey.

Soon after this, the black cliffs of Antalya come into view

Eternal flames at Yanartaş

Antalya

Described in brochures as the 'Honolulu of Turkey', Antalya is the tourist capital of Mediterranean Turkey. It has long sweeping beaches, unpolluted waters and is surrounded on three sides by snowcapped mountains, the Bey Dağları in the west and the Toros Dağları (Taurus Mountains) in the north and east. Built on cliffs that plunge suddenly into the Mediterranean, it is a garden city with big public parks and masses of palm trees. It also lies on the edge of a vast fertile plain known in antiquity as Pamphylia.

The city was founded by Attalus II, king of Pergamum (159–136 BC), during the early days of his rule and named Attaleia after him. It was then ruled successively by the Romans and the Byzantines. During the Crusades, the port was used as a springboard for Crusader raids against Muslims in the eastern Mediterranean. It was then conquered by the Seljuk Turks in 1207 and subsequently ruled by their vassals. In 1361 Peter de Lusignan, the king of Cyprus, captured the city, but it finally fell to the Ottoman Turks in 1391.

In 1919, the Italian army occupied Antalya after the defeat of the Ottoman Empire by the Allies in World War I. The Italians withdrew in 1921 when the Turkish nationalists, under Kemal Atatürk, put up armed resistance to the allied occupation.

The first itinerary in this section of the guide concentrates on the city of Antalya itself and the second explores the coast east to Alanya, another popular resort.

Antalya

This afternoon walk, beginning at Kaleiçi, explores the mosques, tombs and museums of the Old Quarter. It takes in a carpet shop, where you can watch the weavers, and concludes with dinner in the marina.

One of the most charming places to stay in Antalya is the Kaleiçi Old Quarter where you can choose from many delightful, modestly priced pensions or small hotels. You can reach this district by car, taking the modern road downhill from Cumhuriyet Bulvarı (there is a public park just above the marina where you must leave your car).

The city is compact and you can see most of its historical sites in a day's walk. After settling into your hotel, take a stroll around the town. Start at Kaleiçi and walk down to the marina, a former fisherman's wharf, now a bustling port with many yachts, schooners and motorboats. When you reach the marina, try some *ajur*, locally produced long juicy cucumbers, and *frenk* yemişi, a refreshing cactus fruit that tastes like a cross between watermelon and cantaloupe and is said to help dissolve kidney stones.

Walk uphill from Iskele Caddesi, a narrow winding street with many souvenir shops. One shop with a courtyard sells handmade **Döşemeatlı carpets**, and young girls can be seen at work on the looms. Döşemeatlı carpets get their name from the village near Antalya where they are produced.

On one street corner you may notice a man selling locally produced teas, spices and edibles. Buy some aromatic *ada çayı* (island tea), *dağ çayı* (mountain tea), or *papatya çayı* (dandelion tea) and *tirmis*, an edible that looks like corn but tastes like hazelnuts.

Soon you come to one of the main squares of Antalya, the **Kaleiçi Square**, with its **Clock**

The Fluted Minaret

Tower, once a part of the ancient city walls. To your left is the **Yivli Minare** (Fluted Minaret), a tower built with red bricks that today is the symbol of Antalya. The 37-metre (120-ft) high tower was constructed in 1230 by Alaeddin Keykubat, a Seljuk Sultan. The original mosque to which it was attached was destroyed and replaced in 1373 by the **Alaeddin Mosque**.

Just south of the Fluted Minaret, toward the marina, is the **Karatay Medresesi**, an Islamic religious school constructed in 1250 by a Seljuk notable. Near it, but on higher ground, are two tombs: **Zincirkıran Mehmed Paşa Türbe**, built in 1378, and the **Nigâr Hatun Türbe**, constructed in 1502. The two Islamic theological seminaries nearby, **Atabey Armağan Medresesi** and the **Ulu Cami Medresesi**, are in ruins.

Exhibit in Antalya Museum

Now walk back to the Clock Tower. Immediately behind it is the 17th-century **Tekeli Mehmet Paşa Mosque**. The mosque is unique because the **Son Cemaat Yeri** (the last place of assembly) is covered by domes inside rather than outside. Foreigners are allowed to enter the mosques, but must remove their shoes at the entrance. Women must cover their hair and arms with scarves.

Cumhuriyet Bulvarı, which eventually becomes Orgeneral Kenan Evren Bulvarı, runs on an east-west axis through the city. Turn left at the clock tower and walk along the street, which is the main shopping district lined with chic clothing stores and fancy seafood restaurants. To your left is the Mediterranean with the Beydağları on the horizon. As you walk up, you come to **Cumhuriyet Meydanı** (Republic Square) with the big equestrian statue of Kemal Atatürk, founder and first President of the Turkish Republic.

About 2½ miles (4km) down this street (on Orgeneral Kenan Evren Bulvarı), near the Konyaaltı Beach, is the **Antalya Museum**, which has a rich collection of prehistoric artifacts from the Beldibi and Karain caves, statuary from the Greek, Hellenistic and Roman periods, and ethnographic displays of clothing and tents used by the nomadic Yörük Turks, who inhabit the surrounding mountains during the summer and the plain in the winter. Two futuristic-looking five-star hotels have opened nearby: the **Sheraton Voyager Hotel** and the **Falez Hotel**.

Return to the Clock Tower and continue to Atatürk Caddesi, an avenue that cuts Cumhuriyet Bulvarı on a north-south axis. There are a number of *lokanta* (modest restaurants) in alleys near the in-

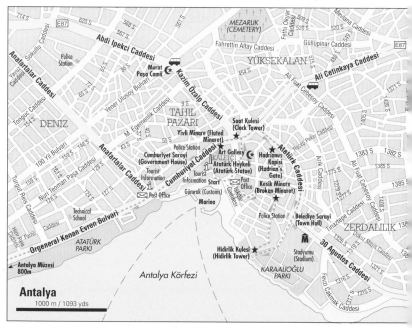

Cooling off in the park

tersection. Turn right at Atatürk Caddesi. You will quickly come upon **Hadrian's Gate** (Hadrianus Kapısı), a magnificent three-arch marble gate erected in AD130 in honour of the Roman emperor's visit to the city.

Continue along the street to the **Belediye** Sarayı (Town Hall) and enter Karaalioğlu Park, lined with palm trees, which offers pleasant outdoor coffeehouses and stunning views.

Walk to the eastern end of the park and you come to the pleasant **Mermerli Coffee House** and the **Hıdırlık Kulesi**, a rotund tower that is believed to be a tomb of a Roman senator from Antalya. Walk up the street that intersects the tower to the **Kesik Minare** (the Broken Minaret). This odd structure stands next to the **Korkut** or **Cumanin Mosque**, now in complete ruins. Built originally in the 5th century as the Panaghia Church, it was converted into a mosque and destroyed in the 19th century.

From the Kesik Minare, walk back to the marina for dinner. Try the **Hisar Restaurant** in the Old Quarter for a combination of Turkish dishes and seafood. After dinner, go to **Club 29 Bar** in the marina for drinks and dancing.

14. A Drive to Alanya

A drive to the resort of Alanya, stopping to explore Perge, Aspendos and Side ruins; trout lunch at Manavgat Falls; swimming at Alanya's golden beaches.

Leave Antalya around 9am and take the main highway to Alanya going east-bound on Cumhuriyet Bulvarı and Sudi Turel Caddesi.

Your first destination is **Perge**, on a road forking off the Antalya–Alanya highway, 20km (12 miles) from Antalya. Turn left at the yellow sign saying Perge. The first building you drive past as you enter Perge is a 2nd-century AD Roman amphitheatre with a seating capacity for 17,000 people. The main ruins are less than a mile from the amphitheatre. Park your car and walk past the stadium, one of the best preserved in the eastern Mediterranean. The 234-metre by 34-metre (765-ft by 110-ft) stadium could seat about 12,000 people. The vaulted sections on the sides of the stadium were originally shops.

The main city, just off the stadium,

Gateway at Perge

was once encircled by walls (some of which are still standing) punctuated by 30 towers. The city was laid out in a grid pattern with two main intersecting streets. You enter the ruins by the **Later Gateway** and arrive at the **City Gate Complex**, a horseshoe-shaped courtyard flanked by two towers. This area is the most fascinating part of the city. Niches built inside the complex walls contained statues of gods and local heroes, such as Mopus and Clacas, the mythic founders of the city. Just behind this complex is the **Monumental Gateway**, a three-arched structure of two storeys, which was also adorned with statues. To the right of the circular courtyard is the **agora**, the city's main shopping centre.

Arcaded street

The main thoroughfare of Perge is a colonnaded street with a water channel, running through the Later Gateway and the City Gate Complex. The water was brought to the city from a source on higher ground. About halfway up this avenue on the left is the **Church of Perge**, which was once a bishopric. At the end of the street, past the intersection, near the acropolis hill, is a **Nymphaion**. If you turn left at the intersection, you come first to a gymnasium, then a bathhouse. A necropolis of several tombs lies at the end of this street.

Perge's early history is unclear. It is believed to have been founded by Greek migrants after the Trojan Wars. When Alexander the Great arrived in Pamphylia in the 4th century BC, the Pergaeans submitted without a struggle. Alexander used Perge as a base for mop-

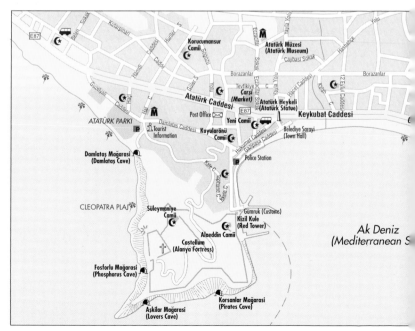

Aspendos Amphitheatre

ping up operations on the coast of southwest Asia Minor. The city was probably abandoned after the 7th-century Arab invasions.

Leave Perge and return to the highway, driving in the direction of Alanya. Your next destination is **Aspendos**, located near the village of Belkız, about 50km (30 miles) from Antalya. Take the road signed Aspendos that forks to the left. The road continues over the **Köprüçay** (the Eurymedon river) for about 5km (3 miles). The first ruins you'll see are the remains of two public baths. Next is the great **Aspendos Amphitheatre**, the world's most magnificent ancient theatre. As many as 20,000 people can be accommodated. The theatre, which is used today to stage the **Antalya Opera and Ballet Festival** in June, has excellent acoustics. Test them by walking up to the very top gallery of the theatre and get someone to whisper from the stage below or even drop a pin.

Spend about half an hour exploring the theatre. In the vicinity of the stadium are some sarcophagi and tombs, including one hewn out of the rocks. An acropolis behind the amphitheatre can be entered through three gates, of which the northernmost is best preserved though half-buried. The structures include an agora, a market hall with several shops intact, a 3rd-century AD basilica, a nymphaion, a council chamber and an aqueduct.

After exploring Aspendos, return to the Alanya highway by

Alanya

1000 m / 1093 yds

crossing over the stone Köprüçay Bridge, built in the 13th century by the Seljuk Turks. The bridge is narrow, but sturdy, and can accommodate one car at a time.

The next stop is the resort village of **Side**, a captivating settlement next to the ruins of one of the oldest and most impressive ancient settlements in Turkey. The ruins are situated on a peninsula 80km (50 miles) from Antalya. To get there, turn right at the yellow sign showing Side near a service station before reaching the town of **Manavgat**. From here it is a short drive to Side.

The proximity of an inhabited village to the ancient ruins adds a romanticism to the site. To get the full visual impact, visit Side between November and March, when there are very few tourists. In summer, Side is crowded with visitors and its hotels and pensions are fully booked.

Side, which means 'pomegranate', is a pre-Greek word that symbolised fertility. The city is believed to have been founded by migrants in the 13th or 14th century BC. In the 6th century, the city was dominated by the Lycians and then the Persians. It was conquered by Alexander the Great in 334BC, and later controlled by the Ptolemites and the Seleucids. Between 188 and 78BC, the Kingdom of Pergamum gained hegemony over the city, transforming it into an important port, the remains of which can still be seen today. It became a Graeco-Roman city, and an important Christian centre but was abandoned in the 12th century. The present inhabitants of Side are the descendants of Turkish refugees who fled Crete during the uprising of 1898 and settled in this village.

Tomb in Side museum

Side was made world-famous by the late Alfred Friendly, former managing editor of the *Washington Post* and Pulitzer Prize winning American journalist who lived here for many years. A foundation set up by Friendly's wife has helped finance the restoration of many sites in Side, including the temples by the harbour.

The first ruins you see as you enter Side are the aqueducts, the remains of city walls and a nymphaion. Suddenly the **Side Amphitheatre** looms up before you on the left, next to the agora. Across is the **Bathhouse Museum**. You will drive past the **Vespasian Monument** and enter the city through the **Later City Gate**, an arched entrance, inside which you must leave your car in the car park.

Now walk down the main street of the village to the harbour, once the commercial hub of Pamphylia and now a simple fisherman's cove. To your left are the **Temple of Apollo** and the **Temple of Athena**, both dating from the 2nd century AD, and a 9th-century Byzantine basilica. Walk along the shore east of the town to the **Temple of Men**, a moon goddess (you will see a crescent-shaped sandy

Manavgat Falls

beach). Soon you come to the **State Agora** and **M-Building**, which resembles a palace.

Most of the walls around the city are either submerged in sand or partly sunken in the sea. From the state agora, find the amphitheatre and walk to the top rows of seats to get a stupendous view of Side. From there walk to the Bathhouse Museum, an ancient bath that has been restored and turned into a museum. It contains many fine Roman statues and sarcophagi, including several in the courtyard.

Now leave Side for Manavgat Falls to have lunch. Return to the highway and turn toward Alanya. You will soon come to the market town of **Manavgat**. A road sign showing **Manavgat Şelalesi** (Falls) and **Oymapınar Barajı** (Dam) forks to the left. If you travel on this road for 17km (10 miles), it will lead you to the Oymapınar Dam, one of the biggest hydro-electric dams in Turkey.

Five kilometres (3 miles) up the road is the turnoff for the Manavgat Falls. Turn right and park your car, then walk to the falls, where you will find several restaurants serving *alabalık* (trout), *piliç shish* (chicken on a skewer) or *piliç çevirme* (barbecued chicken) and tasty appetisers. The **Manavgat River** is one of Turkey's main sources for trout fishing. It is also only one of the few places in Turkey where river rafting has been tried by sports enthusiasts.

After lunch, return to the Alanya road. Alanya is about 51km (30 miles) from Manavgat. The road hugs the shore, and you will notice fine deserted beaches along the way, including the **Incekum Beach**. Halfway to Alanya, you pass a 13th-century Turkish caravanserai, **Serafsahan**, on your left.

Alanya is built around a rocky peninsula. Jutting out to the sea

Alanya bay

Alanya's Red Tower

like an immense mollusc, the red peninsula is crowned by a long crenellated fortress built by the Seljuk Turks in the 13th century to guard this section of the Mediterranean coast. In ancient times, the peninsula served as the headquarters of Pamphylian pirates who raided passing commercial ships for booty and slaves. Alanya was called **Coracesium** in antiquity, the town that that the love-struck Mark Antony purchased for Cleopatra.

Alanya has some of the finest beaches in Turkey and you will probably want to spend an hour or more swimming and tanning on the long beach just before town. Afterwards drive to the **Damlataş Cave,** on the edge of the peninsula, before entering the city. The damp air inside this claustrophobic cave with its thousands of colourful calcified stalactites is believed to benefit sufferers from asthma and other respiratory diseases (but elderly people with heart ailments should avoid it).

Drive into Alanya after your visit to the cave. Located at the foot of the peninsula, Alanya has many seaside restaurants.

Alanya is known among Turks as 'Little Germany' because of the tens of thousands of German holidaymakers who visit it annually. The town's symbols are the 13th-century **Red Tower** (Kızıl Kulesi), a crenellated defensive building, and the ancient **shipyards** which are near the harbour. You will visit these later on.

Next drive up the hill to the fortress, perched on top of the peninsula at a dizzying height of 243m (800ft), overlooking the town and the majestic cliffs that plunge steeply into the sea. The ancient walls around the old city wind 7km (4 miles) uphill, like the Great Wall of China, to the citadel, known as **Içkale**, capped by three towers.

Old Quarter residents

Inside is a courtyard with a Byzantine church and a pleasant outdoor coffeehouse where you can take a break.

You can usually see men here selling dolls fashioned from squashes, a particular art in this part of Turkey. At the northeastern corner of the courtyard is **Adam Atacağı** ('the place from which men are thrown'). It was from here that condemned men were hurled down the cliffs to their deaths. According to one legend, a condemned man would be pardoned only if he could toss a pebble from that height into the sea – an impossible task. Next to here is a deep open pit covered by railings which may have served as a dungeon for prisoners.

From the citadel, you can look down at **Cilvarda Burnu**, a rocky promontory on which there are the ruins of three buildings, including the town's mint (**Darphane**), a tower and a monastery complex. The only way to reach these buildings is to take a boat along the peninsula from Alanya to the promontory and walk up.

Before you drive back to Alanya, visit the inhabited **Old Quarter** of the city in the middle section of the citadel. A left turn as you are about to leave the citadel will take you there, passing the fortress known as the **Ehmedek**. In the Old Quarter, look out for the **Akçebe Sultan** (Small Mosque) and **Türbe** (Tomb). These structures, built in 1230 by the Seljuk Sultan Alaeddin Keykubat I, consist of three sections, two of which contain tombs.

Other buildings of note in this quarter are the **Mecdüddin Cistern**, which is still in use, a caravanserai (inn), comprising a rectangular courtyard surrounded by sleeping quarters, a depot and the **Bedesten** (a shopping centre). Nearby is the **Alaeddin Mosque**, a 13th-century structure that was reconstructed by Süleyman the Magnificent in the 16th century.

Return to Alanya. The first place to stop at is **Bamyacı Ice Cream Parlour** (Güler Pınarı Mahalesi, Keykubat Mevkii), which serves the best ice cream in Turkey. Kemal Bamyacı, who has operated the parlour for decades, offers a range of flavours, as well as sherbets. Afterwards, walk to the Kızıl Kule, a five-storey, 33-metre- (110-ft-) high

Along the quay

octagonal tower which now houses the **Ethnographical Museum**, exhibiting *yörük* tents, rugs and armour. Walk further down to the Shipyards (Tersane) nearby. Used by Seljuks to build their fleet, the shipyards are still used today to construct small boats.

Drive back to Antalya in the early evening. For dinner, head for **Yedi Mehmet Restaurant**, near Konyaaltı Beach, for authentic Turkish food in a convivial atmosphere. Afterwards, relax over a coffee in the Kaleiçi district.

Shopping

Shops on the Turkish Coast offer a dazzling range of large and small mementoes of Turkey, from hand-woven carpets to leather jackets and intricate gold and silver puzzle rings to *meerschaum* pipes. Other souvenirs include leather sandals, worry beads, copperware, ceramic tiles and sponges. All these make great gifts, as well as souvenirs, and many Americans and Europeans who visit the coast in the autumn do their Christmas shopping here.

Handwoven Carpets

Handwoven carpets and flatweaves (another name for kilims) can be good investments as well as souvenirs. Admired worldwide, Turkish hand-woven coverings – for walls, floors, even tables – are the country's best known exports.

For walls and floors

The number of knots per square centimetre is a guide to the quality of the carpet; the more knots, the finer the weave, and generally speaking the stiffer the carpet backing, but tastes vary: some people prefer the tightly woven, soft and flexible carpets. A silk carpet may have between 100 knots per sq cm and 900 knots per sq cm. Wool carpets will have fewer, with an average 36 knots per sq cm. Silk carpets cost much more than wool or cotton carpets.

You can buy carpets all over the Turkish Coast, but the best selection is undoubtedly offered by the Ildız Carpet Farm, near Bodrum, 10 km (6 miles) from Milas. Set up by the Ildız Company, a large producer and carpet exporter, it is probably the world's only carpet farm. At the farm, experts wash and dry under the sun tens of thousands of handmade wool carpets manufactured or bought by the Ildız Company, an Istanbul-based concern which owns the Tribal Art Carpet Shops chain. The 6.8-ha (17-acre) farm is capable of drying as many as 20,000 carpets at one time. The best time to visit is in the early summer when carpets are spread out on the ground, like a huge colourful mosaic. The carpets can be purchased.

Metalware, Meerschaum Pipes and Ceramics

In Marmaris, the **Bazaar 54** carpet shop (Netsel Marina) offers the widest choice of carpets, particularly silk. It also sells all kinds of copper and pewterware, including plates, food trays and wall ornaments, as well as meerschaum pipes and ceramics.

Whether or not you smoke tobacco, meerschaum pipes make unusual table decorations. Turkey is the largest producer of meerschaum, or 'sea foam', a white magnesium silicate. It is mainly produced in Eskişehir in western Anatolia, where hundreds of craftsmen carve the soft mineral into pipes in the shapes of unusual figurines, including turbaned Ottoman sultans and well-known world politicians, such as Bill Clinton and Helmut Köhl. Most larger gift shops sell the pipes, including Bazaar 54 in Marmaris and the Lapis chainstore in Kuşadası and Alanya.

Colourfully decorated ceramic plates, tiles cups and vases are sold all along the Turkish

Ornamental ceramics Coast. Produced mainly in Kütahya, in Anatolia, they can be used decoratively or as tableware.

Prayer beads and intricate gold and silver puzzle rings are among the best jewellery buys, but you should learn how to put a puzzle ring together before leaving the shop. Handmade gold and silver jewellery, including bracelets, rings and brooches, are cheaper in Turkey than in Europe because labour is less expensive. Special blue beads said to ward off the 'evil eye' are also common.

Edibles

There are lots of possibilities here, from tins of honey to spices such as saffron, and bags of pine nuts, *tirmis* and pecans. Especially hard to resist are the ubiquitous Turkish delight and gift-wrapped boxes of honey-oozing pastries such as *baklava*.

Sponges

Turkey continues to be the world's biggest producer of commercial bath sponges, which make very welcome gifts. Sponge diving is an important means of livelihood for many Turks on the coast, especially in and around Bodrum.

Porous marine animals, sponges are found at depths of 10 metres (33ft) to 70 metres (234ft), though some are found at much greater depths. There are more than 5,000 known varieties in the world, mostly marine. A few varieties live in fresh waters.

Known in Turkey as *sünger*, sponges vary in shapes and size and may reach a diameter of 1 metre (3ft).

Ottoman-style ewers

Eating Out

Turkish cooking is one of the finest cuisines in the world. Based on the heritage of the vast Ottoman Empire, which spread from Vienna in the northwest to the southern tip of the Arabian Peninsula, and from the Caspian Sea in the east to the Sahara Desert in the west, it is extremely diverse. The resorts of Bodrum, Marmaris, Fethiye and Antalya offer Turkish and international cuisine restaurants as well as seafood *lokantas* (modest traditional eateries). Bodrum and its environs alone have more than a dozen genuinely international restaurants, including Chinese, Thai, French, Italian, Mexican, British, etc. It also offers some of the best Turkish Mediterranean cuisine and seafood in the country.

Bodrum

The best Turkish cuisine restaurant is the **Han Restaurant** (Kale Caddesi 23, tel: 0252-3167951), set in an old *han* (Ottoman inn). Customers can stand up and do the *çifteteli*, a kind of belly dance, accompanying the professional female dancers.

One of the best Chinese Restaurants is **Salmakis Chinese Restaurant** (Cumhuriyet Cad 8, tel: 0252-3161090). Another is the **Far East Chinese Restaurant** (Neyzen Tevfik Caddesi 146, tel: 0252-3165541), with a view of the harbour. Other ethnic restaurants are: **Ladda's** (Neyzen Tevfik Caddesi, tel: 0252-3131504) for Thai cuisine; **Picante** (Kulcu Sokak 8, tel: 0252-3160270) for Mexican food and good *margaritas*; **Pancho's** (opposite Halikarnas Disco, tel: 0252-3160893) for Argentinian-style steaks; **Sunny's** (Cumhuriyet Caddesi, tel: 0252-3160716) and **Old Stone House** (on Hamam Sokak) for a British menu.

At **Kortan** (Cumhuriyet Caddesi 32, tel: 0252-3162141), try an array of seafood salads, such as octopus salad marinated in lemon juice and olive oil, pickled sea bream, shrimp salads, and *kalamar* (fried squid). **Amphora** (Neyzen Tevfik Caddesi 172, tel: 0252 3162368) is another possibility, serving assorted seafood at moderate prices.

Good seafood places abound in villages near Bodrum, such as Gümüşlük, Yalıkavak,Türk-

Fresh fish abounds

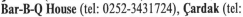

bükü and Bitez. Some of the best restaurants outside Bodrum town are **Alarga** (tel: 0252-3775006) and **Mey** (tel: 0252-3775118) both in Türkbükü, **Alina** (tel: 0252-3854803) and-**Şamdan** (tel: 0252- 3644424) in Yalıkavak, **Bar-B-Q House** (tel: 0252-3431724), **Çardak** (tel: 0252-3431021) and **Salmakis Chinese** in Bitez, and **Batı** (tel: 0252-3943079) in Gümüşlük.

Marmaris

The best Turkish restaurant is **Birtat** (Barbaros Caddesi, near the marina, tel: 0252-4121076). For pizza try **Napoli** (Barbaros Caddesi, Barlar Sokak 70, tel: 0252-4126555). Among the fish restaurants **Yakamoz** (Kemeralti Selen Otel Karsisi, tel: 0252-4125160) is a dependable choice, as is **Baba'nın Yeri** (Baba's Place), among the ruins of Knidos. Have the proprietor cook *istakoz* – lobster.

Fethiye

Try **Happy Chinese Restaurant** (next to the marina) where you can get first-rate Chinese cuisine at reasonable prices, **L'Angolo Italiano** (Neyzen Tevfik Caddesi, Yalı Cikmazı), an inexpensive Italian eatery, **Pizza 74** (Atatürk Caddesi 4, tel: 0252-6141869), the best Italian restaurant in Fethiye. For fish, try **Rafet Restaurant** (Kordonboyu 8–9, tel: 0252-6141106), whose proprietor Rafet Tuna serves delicious *orfoz* (dusky grouper) and *akya* (leer fish). Another excellent, but expensive, fish restaurant is **Meğri** (Likya Sokak 8–9, tel: 0252-6144046), while **Amfora** (Paspatur Hamam Sokak 5, tel: 0252-6121282) specialises in fish baked in salt.

Apricots – a good local buy

Antalya

Fine Turkish and international cuisine restaurants include **Kırkmerdiven** (Kaleiçi, Musalla Sokak 2, tel: 0242-2429686) which offers a cosy fireplace in winter, **Marina Hotel**'s restaurant and **La Notte** (both on Mermerli Sokak). Other select restaurants include the nearly century-old kebab institution of **Develi** (Akdeniz Bulvarı, Birinci Arap Suyu 1, Konyaaltı, tel: 0242-2291200); **Club 29** (above the marina, Kaleiçi, tel: 0242-2416260) which has a superb view of the harbour from its ritzy terrace, as well as Turkish and international food; **Yedi Memet** (Konyaaltı Beach, tel: 0242- 2411641) which combines kitsch decor and excellent Turkish cuisine; **Kral Sofrası** (Yacht Marina 35, tel: 0242-2412198) serving delicious regional *mezes*, fish and meat in a cosy ambience; **Hisar** (Cumhuriyet Meydanı, Tophanealtı, tel: 0242-2415281) in the old fortress; and the gourmet **La Trottoria** Italian restaurant (Fevzi Çakmak Caddesi 3/C, tel: 0242-2433931.

Calendar of Special Events

The following festivals punctuate a year on the Turkish Coast:

January

Every year in mid-January, the market town of Selçuk hosts the Super Bowl of camel wrestling, the Selçuk Camel Wrestling Festival (check with the Selçuk Tourist office for exact dates, tel: 0232-8926945 or 8926328). For two days an atmosphere of carnival excitement prevails in the town as the top male fighting camels of Turkey vie for honors, prize money and trophies in the ruined stadium at Ephesus, in Roman times the venue for gladiator fights and baiting Christians. Thousands of peasants descend on the town from nearby villages for the tournament, not only to bet on their favourite camels but also to sell their produce, carpets and other handicrafts to the crowds.

Turkey's 250 best fighting camels are known as *tülüs*. Weighing over a ton and standing around 1.8 metres (6ft) at the shoulders and 2.3 metres (7ft 6 inches) from the top of the hump, these camels can earn their owners up to $1,200 for each bout, plus much more on side bets.

More than 120 top camels slug it out in this annual extravaganza. Two snorting, bellowing male *tülüs* are brought in and placed at opposite ends of the stadium. Action begins when a female camel is sent strutting betwee the two rivals to arouse their excit ment and ire. Suddenly the two came charge at one another like angry bul butting heads, bumping sides, kic ing with their feet, and often goi into a dangerous neck lock or leg loc The stronger animal tries to crush h opponent with its weight.

Each bout lasts about 10 minute after which two teams of men, ea with nine members, pull the anima apart in a tug-of-war. No animals a seriously hurt: the only injuries a bruises and bloody noses. The mo exciting matches are among the t heavyweights.

In order to win, one camel has knock its oponent down on its sid chase it out of the stadium or cau it to squeal a camel's version of 'su render'. Otherwise the match is deeme a draw. In addition to prize mon and earnings from bets, the anima owner takes home a trophy and priz of handmade carpets.

May/June

The **Kuşadası Music Festival** in Ma has many international pop, jazz ar folk singers. Call the Kuşadası Touris office for information and details c how to book (tel: 0256-6141103; fa 6146295). Even more exciting for son is the annual **Aspendos Opera an Ballet Festival** which takes place in tl ancient theatre in early June. This wel reserved Roman theatre, situated ome 40km (25 miles) east of Antalya, as excellent acoustics. The festival osts celebrated international and Turkish artists, growing more popular every year. Monserrat Caballe and ose Carreras are among the perenial stars. For further information, all Antalya's tourism offices: tel: 242-2411747/2470541/2475042.

Tevfik Caddesi, 4 Bodrum; tel: 0252-3162054, fax: 0252-3165338).

The **Antalya Golden Orange Film Festival** and **Arts Festival** are held in the autumn, usually in late September or early October, when the leading Turkish films of the year are screened and the top films, directors, actors and actresses are awarded the Turkish equivalent of Oscars.

September/October/November

The **Bodrum Cup** takes place in the autumn. It is the only wooden international yacht regatta in which passengers can double as crew if they wish. The regatta is not merely a race but an international yacht festival and the course follows the favourite routes of the Blue Voyage. Its objective is to encourage and expand use of sails among Turkey's fleet of traditional wooden charter yachts known as gulets. Though competing is reserved for wooden yachts, other boats can participate (but cannot take any of the prizes). For more information call: ra Yachting and Tourism (Neyzen

December

Church scholars and amateur historians invade the farming community of Demre (ancient Myra), famed for its red tomatoes and juicy oranges, to attend the **St Nicholas Symposium and Festival,** 1–6 December.

Church services are usually held on 6 December at the Church of Saint Nicholas, where the original Santa Claus served as a priest, the Bishop of Myra, more than 1,650 years ago. In addition to church services, there are performances by the Whirling Dervishes and choral performances. For more information call Kaş Tourism Office, tel: (0242) 8361238.

Camel wrestling

PRACTICAL Information

By Air

Turkish Airlines has a good network of local and international flights. You can fly to Istanbul and take connecting flights to Izmir Adnan Menderes International Airport or Dalaman International Airport; alternatively, fly to Antalya International Airport. In summer, many charter flights operate to these cities directly from Europe. There is no airport tax.

Owners of small planes can fly directly to Imsik Airport, a tiny, privately-owned airstrip near the carpet-producing village of Mumcular, 32km (20 miles) from Bodrum. Imsik has a squadron of 18-person passenger planes with daily flights between Istanbul and Bodrum. Although it is slightly more expensive than domestic Turkish Airlines, Imsik provides direct access to Bodrum.

A Turco-British consortium has built an international airport at Güllük, Milas, a resort 72km (45 miles) from Bodrum.

Turkish Airlines offices on the Turkish Coast: Antalya, tel: (0242) 2434383; Dalaman, tel: (0252) 6925899; Izmir, tel: (0232) 4258280; Bodrum, tel: (0252) 3133172.

By Sea

Turkish Maritime Lines (TML) has a regular boat service from Istanbul to Bodrum, Marmaris and Antalya. TML's Antalya office is on Kenan Evren Bulvarı 40/19, tel: (0242) 2411120/2412630. TML operates a weekly service to Venice from Antalya, between June and October.

A great way to arriv

A regular ferry boat service operate between Bodrum and the Datça Penin sula, south of the Gulf of Gökova, b tween April and October. Ferry boats als operate between Bodrum and Cos, Ma maris, Rhodes, Kuşadası and Samos.

By Bus

There are frequent bus services from I tanbul, Ankara and Izmir to Bodrun Fethiye, Marmaris, Antalya and Alany The Antalya offices of the large, reliab bus companies that serve the Turkish Coa from the major cities of Turkey are: Kam Koç, tel: (0242) 3311170; Pamukkale, te (0242) 3311020; Ulusoy, tel: (024 2421303; Varan, tel: (0242) 2423618.

Climate/When to Visit

Summers are hot and sultry and winte are mild. The best time to visit the ar is May to June and September to Oct ber. It gets unbearably hot from July t August, forcing locals to move to t mountain plateaux for a cooler climate.

verage temperatures for Bodrum are:

.nuary	50°F (10°C)
pril	70°F (21°C)
ıly	88°F (31°C)
ctober	72°F (22°C)

verage temperatures for Antalya are:

.nuary	52°F (11°C)
pril	72°F (22°C)
ıly	90°F (32°C)
ctober	73°F (23°C)

Visas

ationals of Australia, Austria, Finland,
rance, Germany, Greece, Italy, Norway,
letherlands, New Zealand, Spain, Switzer-
.nd and the United States do not require
visa for up to three months. British cit-
ens require a visa, but this can be ob-
.ined on arrival. Nationals of any other
ountries should check with their nearest
urkish consulate.

Vaccinations

s a rule, precautions are not necessary;
ıt if you plan to travel on to central or
.stern Anatolia, cholera and typhoid in-
ctions and a tetanus booster are a good
lea. Malaria tablets are recommended
hen in the Adana area.

Customs

: is forbidden to take antiquities out of
urkey. Persons found to be removing
ıch objects are charged with smuggling.

Clothing

ight clothing is recommended in sum-
ıer, as it can get very hot. From Novem-
.r to March sweaters and overcoats are
ecessary. Comfortable shoes are a must
or visiting archaeological sites, and
omen must wear a head covering (such
; a scarf) when visiting mosques.

Electricity

he electricity in Turkey is 220 volts, 50-
ycle, with two-round prong continental
lugs. British visitors with three-prong
lugs should bring an adaptor.

Time Differences

urkish Standard Time is seven hours
head of Eastern Standard Time and two
ours ahead of Greenwich Mean Time.

Traditional cover-up

MONEY MATTERS

Most banks cash travellers' cheques and
foreign currency. Banking hours are
8.30am–noon and 1.30–5pm, Monday to
Friday. In major resorts one bank usually stays open over the weekends.

The national currency is the Turkish
lira (TL). It comes in coins of 5, 10, 25
and 50,000, and notes of 50, 100, 250,
and 500,000, and 1 and 5 million. Turkey
has an inflation rate of 80–120 percent.

Tipping

A service charge of 10 percent is usually
included in restaurant bills. Waiters, however, expect another 5 percent.

TOURIST INFORMATION

The following is a list of tourist information offices on the Turkish Coast:

ALANYA
*Çarşı Mahallesi, Kale Arkası (behind the
Citadel, opposite the Museum)*
Tel: (0242) 5131240/5135436 (also fax)

ANTALYA
*Selçuk Mahallesi Mermerli Sokak (next to
Ahi Yusuf Mosque, Kaleiçi)*
Tel: (0242) 2475042/2470541/2421833
Fax: (0242) 2476298

*Cumhuriyet Caddesi 91 (next to Turkish
Airlines office)*
Tel: (0242) 2411747/2415271

BODRUM
Iskele Meydanı (at the harbour, near the castle)
Tel: (0252) 3161091; tel/fax: 3167694

DALAMAN
Dalaman Hava Limanı
Tel/fax: (0252) 6925220

DATÇA
Belediye Binası
Iskele Meydanı
Tel/fax: (0252) 7123546

Tourist Information

FETHIYE
Iskele Karşısı, 1 (at the harbour)
Tel/fax: (0252) 6141527

KUŞADASI
Liman Caddesi, 13
Tel: (0256) 6141103
Fax: (0256) 6146295

MARMARIS
Iskele Meydanı (Harbour Square)
Tel: (0252) 4121035
Fax: (0252) 4127277

SELÇUK
Atatürk Mahallesi
Agora Çarşısı 35
Tel/fax: (0232) 8926945

HOURS AND HOLIDAYS

Business Hours

Government offices open from 8.30am–noon and 1.30–5pm. Shops open from approximately 9am–7pm.

Public Holidays

New Year's Day: 1 January
Ramadan (*Şeker Bayramı* or 'sugar eating holiday'): date moves forward each year by 10 days.
National Sovereignty and Children's Day: 23 April

Youth and Sports Holiday: 19 May
The Feast of Sacrifice (*Kurban Bayramı*) date moves forward by 10 days each year.
Victory Day: 30 August
Republic Day: 29 October

HEALTH AND EMERGENCIES

Medical Services

Visitors to Turkey should avoid going to hospitals (*hastane*) for medical treatment except in an emergency. Where possible you are advised to return to your own country for treatment, and should take out insurance to allow for this.

Turkey's hospitals are overcrowded, understaffed and underequipped. Nevertheless, there are many good doctors in private practice, many of whom speak English, French and German.

For minor cuts and infections, buy medication at a dispensary (*dispanser*) or a drug store (*eczane*). Antibiotics can be obtained without a prescription.

Hospitals

Nationwide
SOS INTERNATIONAL *Tel: (0532) 215378*

Bodrum
BODRUM STATE HOSPITAL
(Devlet Hastanesi), Turgutreis Caddesi
Tel: (0252) 3131420

BODRUM CLINIC
Sağlik Ocağı Turgutreis Caddesi
Tel: (0252) 3161353

Antalya
MEDITERRANEAN UNIVERSITY MEDICAL SCHOOL HOSPITAL
Akdeniz Universitesi Tip Fakültesi Hastanesi. Tel: (0242) 2274343

ANTALYA PRIVATE HOSPITAL
Bayındır Mahallesi, 325 Sokak 8
Tel: (0242) 3350000

Alanya
HAYAT HASTANESI PRIVATE HOSPITAL
Yeni Hastane Caddesi
Yayla Yolu Civarı
Tel: (0242) 5121455

Water

Drinking tap water in Turkey, even in luxury hotels, isn't advisable. Bottled water is sold everywhere and is inexpensive.

Security and Crime

Crimes of violence are rare. Pickpocketing is on the rise in crowded resorts. Cars with cassette/radios are also targets.

Drugs

Possession of narcotics, including hashish, is a serious criminal offence and is punished with a long prison sentence.

COMMUNICATIONS AND NEWS

Telephone

Phone calls can be made from the post office (PTT) using tokens (*jeton*) or phone cards. A small jeton can be used for local calls and a big jeton for overseas calls. To call abroad, dial the international access code 00, followed by the country code: Australia (61); France (33); Germany (49); Japan (81); Netherlands (31); Spain (34); UK (44); US and Canada (1). If using a US credit phone card, dial the company's access number – AT&T, tel: 9 (wait second dial tone), then 9 8001 2277; MCI, tel: 9 8001 1177.

Post

Turkish mail service is not always reliable. Send postcards and letters, special delivery (*taahhütlü*). Main post offices (PTT) are open 8am–noon Monday to Saturday, and 9am–7pm Sunday. Smaller post offices are not open on Sundays. Post offices in the main resorts are open 24 hours a day.

Newspapers

Turkey has one English language newspaper: the *Turkish Daily News*, published in Ankara. Major international newspapers, including the *Financial Times*, *The Wall Street Journal* and the *International Herald Tribune* are widely available.

Go your own speed

GETTING AROUND

Dolmuş

The dolmuş is a collective taxi, often a mini-bus, which follows specific routes. Each passenger pays according to the distance travelled: fares are determined by the municipality. Dolmuş connect towns, as well as running shorter distances between villages, and are a very useful and inexpensive way of travelling.

Buses

Turkey has comfortable long-distance bus services, operating both day and night. Coaches are modern and prices inexpensive. Coaches depart from the coach station (*ötogar*) in large towns and from the centre of smaller towns.

Car Rental

Bodrum
Avis, tel: (0252) 3162333/3161996
Budget, tel: (0252) 3167383; fax: 3163078
Hertz, tel: (0252) 3134808
Marmaris
Avis, tel: (0252) 4122771/4126412
Budget, tel: (0252) 4124144
Europcar, tel: (0252) 4122001
Hertz, tel : (0252) 4122552
Fethiye
Avis, tel: (0252) 6146339/6121385
Budget, tel: (0252) 6146166
Antalya
Airtour Rent a Car, tel: (0242) 2483422
Avis, tel: (0242) 2416693/2425642
Budget, tel: (0242) 2433006
Airport Office: (0242) 3303079
Hertz, tel: (0242) 2429929

Helicopter Rentals:

Tours of the region can be made by helicopter. Contact: Doruk Tourism and Travel Agency, Burhanettin Onat Caddesi 92/2, Antalya, tel: (0242) 3210032; fax: 3210924.

Bodrum: capped by its castle

Bodrum

Bodrum has more than 300 pensions as well as several five-star hotels and scores of four and three-star hotels. Accommodation can also be found in coastal villages and towns within 20km (12 miles) of Bodrum. Prices include double room and breakfast for two persons, or breakfast and one meal (half board). The case is indicated at the end of each entry.

$120 AND ABOVE
CESARS
Okaliptus Sokak 4, Gümbet
Tel: (0252) 3169571
On Gümbet Beach, 2km (1 mile) from Bodrum. A 5-star hotel with a pretty garden full of statuettes. Indoor and outdoor pools as well as private beach, fitness centre, casino and restaurants. Half board.

CLUB HOTEL M
Değirmen Mevkii
Tel: (0252) 3166100
On the outskirts of Bodrum, with a private beach. Offers many wet and dry sports, including parachuting, as well as a casino and disco. Half board.

$100 AND ABOVE
AMBRIOSA
Bitez Yalısı
Tel: (0252) 3431886
On the popular windsurfing bay at Bitez village, about 8km (5 miles) from Bodrum, with superb views of the Aegean. Canoeing, windsurfing, waterskiing and banana skiing available. Half board.

ELDORADOR MILTA
Kaynar Mevkii, Bodrum
Tel: (0252) 3671800
Member of a French holiday village chain. Facilities include a private cove, Turkish baths, sailing, windsurfing, tennis and archery. Half board.

MANASTIR
Barış Sitesi
Tel: (0252) 3162854
Away from the bustling crowds, yet within the city limits, Manastır has a commanding view of Bodrum Castle and the harbour. Set on a small hill, it has no beach but a pleasant pool, with poolside bar and restaurant to compensate. Half board.

$80 AND ABOVE
ANTIQUE THEATRE
Kıbrıs Şehitleri Caddesi 243
Tel: (0252) 3166053
Situated across from the ancient theatre. Just 19 rooms designed in the traditional Bodrum style. Antique pieces in the flower garden, handmade bedspreads, and candlelit dinners by the poolside add to the charm. Bed and breakfast.

HOTEL SAMI
Gümbet Beach, near Bodrum
Tel: (0252) 3161048
One of the most popular hotels on this large, sandy beach, Sami is built on terraced grounds, offering sea views, a beach barbecue restaurant, sun terrace, pretty pool and daily boat excursions. Half board.

$50 AND ABOVE
BITEZ HAN
Bitez Yalısı
Tel: (0252) 3431766
On the beach in Bitez village. An inexpensive hotel with 80 rooms, watersports, Turkish bath and pool. Half board.

MYNDOS
Mindos Caddesi 1
Tel: (0252) 3163080
A small hotel behind the marina. 51 rooms, and a pretty garden with a pool. Open year-round. Bed and breakfast.

$30 AND ABOVE
ARCADE
Cumhuriyet Caddesi 159
Tel: (0252) 3168883
Budget hotel near the centre, with a pleasant terrace overlooking the sea, and a tiny swimming pool. Bed and breakfast.

Marmaris

$150 AND ABOVE
MARTI HOLIDAY VILLAGE
İçmeler
Tel: (0252) 4553440
Seaside setting, attentive service and a host
of sporting and entertainment facilities:
watersports, tennis,Turkish bath, fitness
centre, jacuzzi, live shows, casino, bars,
disco. Half board.

ROBINSON SELECT CLUB MARIS
On the Datça road 30km (19 miles) from
Marmaris, Hisarönü Mevkii
Tel: (0252) 4369200
Perched on a high hill above a secluded
cove, Robinson has sweeping views of the
Aegean, and an all-inclusive price of
around $190. Sports facilities include cata-
maran sailing, diving, waterskiing, surf-
ing, canoeing, tennis, and a health and
beauty centre. Full board.

$100 AND ABOVE
MERIT GRAND AZUR
Kenan Evren Bulvarı 11
Tel: (0252) 4128201
A large, five-star hotel on the waterfront,
not far from the city centre. Has a large
pool with water slides, and a jacuzzi. Also
has entertainment, gourmet restaurants,
casino, and nightclub. Half board.

TURUNÇ
Turunç Köyü
Tel: (0252) 4767024
In pretty Turunç village, 23km (14 miles)
east of Marmaris town, this is a large hotel set along a wood-backed beach. Many
sports are available, including scuba diving, jetskiing and parachuting. Half board.

$70 AND ABOVE
MAGIC LIFE DER CLUB KNIDOS
On the road to Datça, Çabucak Köyü
Tel: (0252) 4666434
Set alongside a secluded bay on the Datça
Peninsula. A large hotel in lush grounds.
Offers full board accommodation at rea-
sonable prices, including a scuba diving
school, football, tennis, watersports, Turk-
ish bath, and colourful live shows. All in-
clusive price.

$60 AND ABOVE
PORTOFINO
Kayabalı Caddesi 84, İçmeler
Tel: (0252) 4553601
Small, pretty hotel set in lush woods, about
7km (4 miles) from Marmaris city centre.
A short walk from the beach. Half board.

$35 AND ABOVE
KAVALA HOTEL AND APARTMENTS
Turunç Köyü
Tel: (0252) 4767211
Comfortable flats with kitchen and air-
conditioning, plus 38 hotel rooms. Excel-
lent seaside restaurant. About 23km (14
miles) from Marmaris city. Half board.

Backing on to the beach in Marmaris

Fethiye

$200 AND ABOVE
HILLSIDE BEACH CLUB
Kalem Koyu
Tel: (0252) 6148360
Exclusive luxury club hotel which is a
trendy summer respite for fashionable
Turkish and foreign visitors. Its gourmet
dining facilities, classy entertainment, im-
maculate service and see-and-be-seen am-
bience justify the high price. Full board.

$150 AND ABOVE
CLUB TUANA VISTA
Yanıklar Köyü
Tel: (0252) 6336316
A large (244 rooms), luxurious holiday
club in an idylic setting. Full board ac-
commodation to suit every taste and hol-
iday interest.

$100 AND ABOVE
BELCEKIZ BEACH HOLIDAY VILLAGE
Ölüdeniz
Tel: (0252) 6170077
A cluster of tasteful buildings in a relaxed and luxurious atmosphere. Dance bar, adventure club and pool with jacuzzi add to the fun. Half board.

HOTEL MERI
Ölüdeniz
Tel: (0252) 6170001
Overlooking the lagoon. Delicious buffet meals, plus paragliding, riding, diving, waterskiing and canoeing. Half board.

Alanya

$60 AND ABOVE
MONTANA PINE RESORT
Ovacık Köyü, Ölüdeniz
Tel: (0252) 6166366
Set in a pine forest, Montana has charming, wood-trimmed houses, beautiful gardens and pool, and friendly service. It is ideal for families with children. Shuttle bus to the Ölüdeniz Beach. Half board.

CLUB ORKA
Orta Mahalle, Ovacık Köyü
Tel: (0252) 6166810
A 45-room holiday village with two pools, Turkish bath, nightclub/ disco, etc. 4km (2 miles) from Ölüdeniz Beach and 10km (6 miles) from Fethiye. Half board.

$40 AND ABOVE
ARIES
Çalış Plajı
Tel: (0252) 6131100
A large hotel under international man-

agement, Club Aries has friendly service and exceptionally good food in its roof restaurant. Bed and breakfast.

OCAKKÖY HOLIDAY VILLAGE
Ocakköy, Ovacık
Tel: (0252) 6166155
30 stone cottages built around a 150-year-old Greek village 5km (3 miles) from the beach. Rooms have en-suite bathroom, fan and refrigerator. Perfect for families with children. Also caters for disabled guests. Bed and breakfast.

TELMESSOS
Hisarönü, Ölüdeniz
Tel: (0252) 6166888
3km (2 miles) from Ölüdeniz lagoon. Inexpensive, fun-filled resort-style hotel with a large pool. Bed and breakfast.

$25 AND ABOVE
ST NICHOLAS PARK
Hisarönü, Ölüdeniz
Tel: (0252) 6166288
A good choice for budget travellers. No beach but a pool, jogging and riding grounds. Bed and breakfast.

VILLA DAFFODIL
Karagözler, Fevzi Çakmak Caddesi 115
Tel: (0252) 6149595
Pretty Ottoman-style mansion with 15 rooms, 1km from the centre. Has a pool, sauna, restaurant/bar. Bed and breakfast.

Antalya and Kemer
In and around Antalya city are hotels for every taste and budget. For many, however, the most interesting place to stay is Antalya's Old Quarter – 'Kaleiçi' – inside the ramparts. Many of its old houses are now 'special licence' hotels – small hotels with modern amenities at an inexpensive price.

$150 AND ABOVE
FALEZ
Konyaaltı, Antalya
Tel: (0242) 2485000
Towering above Konyaaltı Beach, Falez offers everything from a laser-show disco to parachuting and archery. Bed and breakfast.

Night bazaar

CLUB TURTLE'S MARCO POLO
Çamyuva, near Kemer
Tel: (0242) 8246336
Large, friendly holiday village where everything from meals and beverages to activities is included in the price.

$100 AND ABOVE
FAVORI AQUA RESORT
Çamyuva, near Kemer
Tel: (0242) 8246214
Small complex with a private beach. Pool with water slides. Half board.

KIRIŞ WOLD MAGIC
Kemer
Tel: (0242) 8246800
A large five-star hotel complex on a long sandy beach. Half board.

RENAISSANCE RESORT
Beldibi, near Kemer
Tel: (0242) 8248431
A large complex surrounded by pine forests and lovely gardens. Half board.

CLUB HOTEL SERA
Lara Yolu, Antalya
Tel: (0242) 3493434
Full of tropical trees and plants. Offers tennis courts, Turkish bath, disco and casino. Half board.

TALYA
Fevzi Çakmak Caddesi 30, Antalya
Tel: (0242) 2486800
The only five-star hotel in the city centre with a private beach. Gourmet restaurants and modern business facilities. Bed and breakfast.

$50 AND ABOVE
ALP PAŞA
Barbaros Mahallesi, Hesapçı Sokak 30-32, Kaleiçi, Antalya
Tel: (0242) 2475676
Ottoman mansion in the Old Quarter. Pool and restaurant. Bed and breakfast.

DOGAN
Mermerli Banyo Sokak 5, Kaleiçi, Antalya
Tel: (0242) 2418842
Friendly, simple and comfortable. Garden. Bed and breakfast.

LARA
Lara Yolu, Antalya
Tel: (0242) 3492930
Small hotel with pool near Lara beach. Rooms with sea views. Bed and breakfast.

MARINA
Mermerli Sokak 15, Kaleiçi, Antalya
Tel: (0242) 2475490
Handsome hotel housed in three Ottoman buildings. Good food, a courtyard garden, and a small pool. Bed and breakfast.

TÜTAV TÜRKEVI
Mermerli Sokak 2, Kaleiçi, Antalya
Tel: (0242) 2486591
Pretty hotel in the Old Quarter. Booking recommended. Bed and breakfast.

$30 AND ABOVE
VILLA PERLA
Barbaros Mahallesi, Hesapçı Sokak 26, Kaleiçi, Antalya
Tel: (0242) 2489793
Converted from a traditional house. Offers garden shaded by citrus trees, a small pool, and classical Turkish cuisine. Bed and breakfast.

Alanya

$100 AND ABOVE
GRAND KAPTAN
Obagöl Mevkii
Tel: (0242) 5140101
Five-star seaside hotel with a casino. Bed and breakfast.

$50 AND ABOVE
AZAK
Atatürk Caddesi 161
Tel: (0242) 5139155
Small inexpensive hotel in the city centre but close to the beach. Most of its 50 rooms have views. A popular rafting and riding club operates from here. Half board.

Sails for hire

BOTANIK
Okurcalar Köyü
Tel: (0242) 5274850
One of the more expensive hotels in this price bracket. Large pool, parasailing, jet-skiing, canoeing, windsurfing. Half board.

$40 AND ABOVE
BEDESTEN
İçkale
Tel: (0242) 5121234
Built inside a converted caravanseria (traditional lodging place for merchants) on the castle rock. Offers splendid views and a small pool. Half board.

Side and Manavgat

$110 AND ABOVE
ASTERIA
Kumköy, Side
Tel: (0242) 7531830
Five-star hotel near Side centre. Has an oympic-size pool. Half board.

TURTEL SORGUN
Titreyengöl Mevkii, Manavgat
Tel: (0242) 7569300
Holiday village, with tennis courts, beach and entertainment facilities. Half board.

$90 AND ABOVE
DEDEMAN CLUB BLUE WATERS
Manavgat
Tel: (0242) 7569464
Peaceful holiday village with attractive pool. Half board.

NIGHTLIFE

The Turkish Coast comes to life late at night with many nightclubs continuing into the small hours. Most discos shut down at 5am. **Bodrum** is famed for its clubs, pubs, bars and discotheques, the most famous of which is the Halikarnas,

with its outdoor dance floor. The Had Garı is the most glamorous bar in Turkey, renowned for its B-52 cocktails.

Marmaris has a 'bar row' running along the waterfront from the Old Citadel to the marina. At the marina, try Keyif Bar, on the second floor of the marina buildings, from where there is a lovely nighttime view of the town's flickering lights. Bars and nightclubs also abound in **Fethiye**, but the best is the Yasmin (Jasmine), a bar with live music in a 19th-century Turkish-Greek house. Many bars and pubs can be found overlooking the marina in the Old Quarter of **Antalya**.

SPORT

Scuba Diving

Scuba diving is increasingly popular along the Turkish Coast, where sunken shipwrecks, starfish, manta rays and seahorses abound. Bodrum is the centre for diving. Foreigners wishing to dive must be accompanied by an authorised Turkish diving guide and can dive only within posted legal boundaries. It is strictly forbidden to dive in the vicinity of ancient shipwrecks, without permission from local and provincial authorities. Diving near a shipwreck without a permit could be considered an act of smuggling. Turkish Coast Guard boats patrol the sites.

Before making a dive, be sure your guide is either PADI or CMAS certified and has a Turkish diving licence (Balık Adamı Rehber). Diving schools include:

Bodrum

AEGEAN PRO DIVE CENTER
Neyzen Tevfik Caddesi 174/C
Tel: (0252) 3160737

AQUAMARINE
Neyzen Tevfik Caddesi 214
Tel: (0252) 3135933

AŞKIN DIVING
Paşa Tarlası Caddesi 11
Tel: (0252) 3164247/3169703

MOTIF
Neyzen Tevfik Caddesi 48
Tel: (0252) 3166252

Marmaris

AQUAVISION
Ulusal Egemenlik Caddesi 36/2
Tel: (0252) 4134811

EUROPEAN DIVING CENTER
Marina, İçmeler, near Marmaris
Tel: (0252) 4554733

FEY DIVING CENTER
*Kenan Evren Bulvarı, next to Turban
Holiday Village*
Tel: (0252) 4125681

PROFESSIONAL DIVING CENTER
Sarıalan Mahallesi, Dördüncü Sokak 19/12
Tel: (0252) 4129989

Fethiye

DIVER'S DELIGHT
Atatürk Caddesi 38
Tel: (0252) 6121099

EUROPEAN DIVING CENTER
At the Harbour
Tel: (0252) 6149771

GERMAN DIVING CENTER
Çalış Beach, near Fethiye city
Tel: (0252) 6133113

MARIN DIVING CENTER
Atatürk Caddesi 36, 2nd floor
Tel: (0252) 6149788

Alanya

ACTIVE DIVERS
Iskele Caddesi 80
Tel: (0242) 5128811

Kaş

BARRACUDA
Based at Hotel La Villa
Tel: (0242) 8362144

LYKIA DIVING CLUB
Based at Hotel Lykia
Tel: (0242) 8361270

Yacht Chartering

Bodrum, a boat-building centre since the days of Antony and Cleopatra, and Marmaris are centres for the Mavi Yolculuk (Blue Voyage), a yachting cruise into Gökova Bay and the coves of the Datça Peninsula.

Bodrum and Marmaris are also the home ports for hundreds of local and foreign boats, available for chartering. Boats can be chartered in the following ways:

Flotilla: Several boats sail around the coast, with a lead boat skippered by an experienced sea captain, an engineer to deal with mechanical problems, and a hostess to show you where to dine and get provisions. This type of chartering is designed for experienced sailors unfamiliar with the surroundings.

Bareboat charters: On a bareboat charter you are pretty much on your own. The agency provides no food supplies and you have to stock up often when you stop at a port or village. To skipper such a boat, you need to have a RYA Yachtmaster's or Overseas Helmsman's Certificate.

Charter gulets: These yachts come with a skipper and crew who do all the work, including cooking your meals. This type of hire is obviously the most expensive.

Day trips: Day boat trips are ideal for those who don't want to live on a boat.

Yacht chartering agencies include:

Bodrum

AEGEAN YACHT SERVICES
Paşatarlası Caddesi 21
Tel: (0252) 3161517

BODRUM PRUVA YACHTING
Neyzen Tevfik Caddesi 48/B
Tel: (0252) 3160443

ERA TOUR
Neyzen Tevfik Caddesi 160/A
Tel: (0252) 3162054

FORA YACHTING
Neyzen Tevfik Caddesi 220
Tel: (0252) 3163046

Time to drop anchor

GIZ YACHT SERVICES
Neyzen Tevfik Caddesi 230/A
Tel: (0252) 3168799

NAUTILUS
Neyzen Tevfik Caddesi 224/A
Tel: (0252) 3166835

PUPA YACHTING
Firkateyn Sokak 19
Tel: (0252) 3162398

Marmaris

EKIN TOUR
Iskele Meydanı (at the Harbour Square)
Tel: (0252) 4122552

GINO TOUR
At Netsel Marina
Tel: (0252) 4120676

MENGI YACHTING
Hacı Sabri Sokak No 7/a
Tel: (0252) 4121307

SETUR YATÇILIK
Barbaros Caddesi, 87
Tel: (0252) 4124608

VENÜS YACHTING
Talatpasa Sok, Demirtas Apt 24
Tel:(0252) 4128535

**YESIL MARMARIS TOURISM AND
YACHT MANAGEMENT**
Barbaros Caddesi, 11
Tel: (0252) 4122290

Fethiye

ALESTA YACHTING AND TRAVEL AGENCY
Opposite Marina, Korbey Apartment 21
Tel: (0252) 6122367

LAMA TOURS
Hamam Sokak 3/A
Tel: (0252) 6144964

LIGHT TOURS
Atatürk Caddesi 104
Tel: (0252) 6144757

SIMENA TRAVEL
*Atatürk Caddesi, PTT Santral Sokak,
Urantaş Sitesi*
Tel: 0252- 614 49 57

Antalya

AIR TOUR
*Kızılsaray Mahallesi, 79 Sokak, Emin
Apart. 9/A*
Tel: (0242) 2483422

AKAY TRAVEL
Cumhuriyet Caddesi 54
Tel: (0242) 2431700

FANTAZI MARINE CENTER
*Esentepe, Göynük (between Kemer and
Beldibi on the main road)*
Tel: (0242) 8151833

MAKI TUR
*Tuzcular Mahallesi, Uzun Çarşı Caddesi
16/B, Kaleiçi*
Tel: (0242) 2431402

PAMFILYA
30 (Otuz) Ağustos Caddesi 57/B
Tel: (0242) 2431500

ROSEMARY'S YACHT CHARTER
Kemer Marina
Tel: (0242) 8143404

TANTUR
Atatürk Caddesi 31, Ulusoy Işhanı
Tel: (0242) 4262530

Back to the beach

Hunting and Fishing

ttalya is a paradise for hunters. The Bey
ığları and Taurus Mountains are rich
game birds and wildlife. Travellers come
om all over the world to Antalya to
nt for the ibex (*yaban dağ keçisi*.
out fishing is popular on the **Manavgat**,
ıçayı, Karaçayı and Köprüçayı rivers,
d in the province of Antalya.
For information related to hunting and
hing, contact the **Antalya Hunters As-
ciation**: Avcilar Dernegi, Kilit Is Hanı,
netpaşa Caddesi, Tel: (0242) 2417626.
Hunting parties are also organised by
ırkish **Union of Travel Agencies**
URSAB): Barbaros Mahallesi, Kandiller
eçidi Sokak 8, Kaleiçi, Antalya, tel:
242) 2431996/2431891.

Golf

ne coast's first 18-hole golf course, the
ational Golf Club, opened in 1994 in
elek, east of Antalya. The club also has
driving range and a 9-hole links for be-
nners. Clubs, carts, caddies, etc can be
red, as can a pro for instruction. Reser-
ttions must be made in advance: The Na-
onal Golf Club, Belek, Antalya, tel:
)242) 7254620; fax: (0242) 7254621.

DORA GOLF RESORT
elek, tel: (0242) 7254051

LTIS GOLF HOTEL
elek, tel: (0242) 7254242

ARADISE TATBEACH GOLF HOTEL
elek, tel: (0242) 7254076

Mountain climbing, trekking and caving

ountain climbing and trekking tours can
e arranged through:

AURUS MOUNTAIN SPORTS CLUB
Milli Egemenlik Caddesi 24, 3rd floor,
o: 31, Antalya
el: (0242) 2481391

REK TRAVEL
Kızılsaray Mahallesi, 61 Sokak, Alanya Iş
Merkezi, no: 10-16, Antalya
el: (0242) 2481629
ax: (0242) 2433499

STOP TOURS
Dr. Burhanettin Onat Caddesi, Yılmaz
Sitesi, A Blok, 2nd floor, No: 14, Antalya
Tel: (0242) 3226557

Rafting

Three travel agencies in Antalya offering
rafting tours are:

ALRAFT RAFTING AND RIDING CLUB
Based at Azak Hotel, Alanya
Tel: (0242) 5139155
Fax: (0242) 5131759

MEDRAFT
Konyaaltı Caddesi, Derya Apt. A Blok
68/16, Antalya
Tel: (0242) 2480083
Fax: (0242) 2427118

Skiing

In March and April you can ski at the
mountain resort of Sakhkent ('the Hidden City') and swim in the Mediterranean
on the same day. The ski resort (winter
only) is in the Bey Dağlari, 50km (30
miles) from Antalya. For more information, call Skiing Center, tel: (0242)
2421360, or Saklıkent Mountain Center,
tel: (0242) 4461210, 4461326.

Horse Riding

The Belek resort to the east of Antalya
city and the Kemer area in the west have
trails suitable for beginners and experienced riders. Travel companies such as Stop
Tours (see under 'Trekking') arrange riding expeditions. For a more complete adventure, you could stay in a rustic ranch.

BAGANA RANCH MOTEL
Yukarı Karaman Köyü (on the road to
Telmessos), Antalya
Tel: (0242) 4252270
Fax: (0242) 4252444

ERENDIZ RANCH HOTEL
Aslanbucak Mevkii, Kemer
Tel: (0242) 8143742

NATURLAND COUNTRY PARK
Çamyuva, Kemer
Tel: (0242) 8246214
Fax: (0242) 8246210

Index

ACKNOWLEDGMENTS

Photography Basin Ajansi, Tolan Arlıhan,
Lalepar Aytek, Metin Demirsar,
Ara Güler, Semsi Güner, Hans Höfer,
Ulus Lararasi, Enis Özbank,
Marcus Wilson Smith, Phil Wood
Production Editor Mohammed Dar
Handwriting V Barl
Cover Design Klaus Geisler
Cartography Lovell Johns
Berndtson & Berndtson